THE CARTOONIST'S MUSE

A Guide to Generating and Developing Creative Ideas

MISCHA RICHTER
and
HARALD BAKKEN

CONTEMPORARY
BOOKS

CHICAGO

Library of Congress Cataloging-in-Publication Data

Richter, Mischa, 1910–
    The cartoonist's muse : a guide to generating and developing
creative ideas / Mischa Richter and Harald Bakken.
       p.   cm.
    Includes bibliographical references.
    ISBN 0-8092-3916-7 (paper)
    1. Cartooning.   2. Creation (Literary, artistic, etc.)
I. Bakken, Harald, 1935–   II. Title.
NC1320.R53   1992
741.5—dc20   92-578
                                   CIP

The authors wish to express their appreciation to the staffs of the libraries of the
University of Massachusetts at Lowell and of Harvard University, Cambridge,
Massachusetts.

The 172 drawings by Mischa Richter appeared originally in *The New Yorker* and
were copyrighted © in the years 1943, 1944, 1945, 1946, 1954, 1963, 1965, 1966, and
1973 through 1992 inclusive, by The New Yorker Magazine, Inc.

Published by Contemporary Books, Inc.
180 North Michigan Avenue, Chicago, Illinois 60601
Manufactured in the United States of America
International Standard Book Number: 0-8092-3916-7

Contents

Section 3: Developing and Polishing Funny Ideas

Section 4: Shop Talk About Cartooning

Section 5: Where to Read More

THE CARTOONIST'S MUSE

1
Introduction

Imagine an unlikely situation. You're sitting in a doctor's outer office, waiting for your appointment. The man or woman across the room—a total stranger—looks at you and says, "Make me laugh. I'll give you seven seconds."

What to do?

There's an easy solution. Grab a magazine from the waiting-room table. If you're lucky, the magazine will be no more than forty years old. (Should you find only copies of *Harper's* dated 1875, consider changing doctors.) Flip through the magazine, find a cartoon, show the drawing to your inquisitor, and hope that the cartoonist has done his or her job.

For that is what a modern magazine cartoonist is supposed to do: get a laugh from a total stranger in under seven seconds.

Compared with other humorists, cartoonists have unusual demands made on them. No one else who professionally tries to make people laugh is expected to do it quite so quickly. A stage actor knows that people in the audience will probably give the show a few minutes of attention before they fall asleep. A writer of TV sitcoms can assume that most viewers know the characters and are prepared to laugh at them. A stand-up comic can at least do a buildup to a joke. Not so a cartoonist. A really good cartoon, like a really good chili con carne, will have an aftertaste. But if the funny flavor isn't there immediately, no one will ever savor it.

Cartoonists are either quick or they're dead.

1

If cartoonists are unusual as humorists, they are also unusual as artists. Consider the settings in which a cartoonist will have work exhibited against those of, say, a painter. A successful painter can look forward to having the viewer's first glimpse of a work come in a gallery. A successful cartoonist can look forward to having a viewer's first glimpse of a work come in a doctor's waiting room, on a subway, in a barber's chair, or—to

cite a setting where we suspect more cartoons are seen than most of us in the business would like to admit—in the smallest room of the viewer's house. The ultimate compliment for a painter is to have a painting hung in a museum. The ultimate compliment for a cartoonist is to have a drawing hung on a refrigerator door or an office bulletin board. And cartoonists have to face the fact that a significant portion of their work will at best end up lining the bottom of a bird cage.

Cartoonists are unusual as artists for another reason: they frequently use words as well as pictures. There are modern cartoonists who rely solely on pictures to achieve their effects. This is more true in Europe than in the United States; the captionless cartoon, while still common, may be an endangered species on the American scene. But in most cases a good modern cartoon is not simply a funny picture. Nor is it simply a funny line. It is a marriage of the two. As with all marriages, if either partner is slighted, the union won't work. In the real world of marriage, divorces give at least the lawyers some reason to be happy. But in the world of funny drawings, a bad union pleases no one—artist or viewer. So a cartoonist has to be skilled with words as well as with drawing.

The demands on cartoonists, then, are great, and the responses to their efforts are often ephemeral. Some of us have occasionally wondered why we didn't go into some form of work where the clients are patient and the results are permanent—for example, undertaking. But the rewards of cartooning are in fact enormous. The challenge of brevity guarantees an immediacy of impact on the viewer that no other art form offers. If you've produced a "good one," you know it will get through to the viewer on a visceral level in a way nothing else can. The demand that the cartoonist combine drawing and words allows for a range of mental activity that is exhilarating. The cartoonist *must* let the left brain know what the right brain is doing. The form is totally portable: a cartoonist's work can be seen anywhere, anytime. In cartooning, the imagination can have almost unlimited rein; no grubby demand to adhere to reality constrains a cartoonist. Cartoonists can say things in visual form that can be said in no other way. And, as a side benefit, cartoonists are more often quoted than any other kind of artist. When was the last time somebody said to you, "Let me tell you a really good Vincent van Gogh?"

Most important, cartooning is fun. In the combined total of over seventy years that we've been in the business, we've developed more than sixty thousand ideas for visual humor. We haven't gotten bored yet. Neither have the hundreds of thousands of people who pick up a magazine and thumb through it to look at the cartoons before they read anything else, or the millions of newspaper readers who turn first to the comics section. (One of the nice things about getting into cartooning is that, if you're already one of those people, you can now claim you're only doing required professional reading.) Viewing cartoons is a great pleasure. Creating them is an even greater delight.

This book is for people who want to know how this unique form of humor and art is created. It's for people who would like to draw cartoons and want to learn more about how to do it. But it's also for people who simply *love* cartoons and want to know more about how the warped minds that create these funny drawings work.

For those of you who want to draw cartoons, a few words of explanation about what we're going to offer: because the quality that makes a cartoon unique among drawings is the fact that it's funny, we'll concentrate on how humor is generated in cartooning. We're going to assume that you already have at least a minimal ability to draw. So we won't say much about elementary drawing skills: perspective, angles of vision, facial expressions, etc. Instead, assuming that you have some basic capability with a pen, we'll show you how you can use the visual and verbal tricks of the trade that professionals employ in order to get laughs with a drawing.

We're also going to assume that you have a basic sense of humor and that occasionally you generate at least the germ of an original funny

notion, not necessarily in visual form. No one can give you that basic sense of humor. Certainly we can't. But, assuming that you sometimes come up with an idea for a "good one," we'll show you how professionals come up with a continuous stream of funny ideas, and how you can do the same thing. We'll also show you how professionals take the germ of an idea and turn it into a finished cartoon.

For those of you who simply love cartoons, we ask that you sit back and enjoy. To enter the world of cartooning is to stretch your imagination, to let your fantasies take flight. It's a world where animals can talk, where inanimate objects think deep thoughts, where historical characters utter very modern sentiments, where people say things out loud that most of us only think in private. In short, it's a world where, in the words of Cole Porter, "anything goes." We hope that, as you learn about how cartoonists think, you may find ways to open up your own creativity. And who knows? From time to time, you may also come up with an idea for a "good one."

We've been talking about "cartooning." But, as we will throughout this book, we're really using that word broadly as a synonym for many visual art forms that are designed, at least in part, to elicit a laugh. We'll emphasize magazine cartooning, the field we know best, but we'll also touch on a variety of other forms, including editorial cartoons, comic strips, and spot drawings. We'll be using the idea of a "laugh" broadly here too. Laughs come in all sizes, shapes, and meanings. And so visual humor comes in all sizes, shapes, and meanings. We'll use examples of visual humor designed to get a belly laugh, but we'll also use examples of drawings designed to get a guffaw, a chuckle, a chortle, a raw laugh, a wry laugh, even a despairing laugh. All are legitimate examples of a cartoonist's art.

While the main focus of this book will be on the modern cartooning style as it developed in the twentieth century, we won't limit ourselves to contemporary drawings. There is a theory—we created it, but that's one of the joys of the trade—that the first funny drawing emerged when a caveman sat puzzling over how to prove his originality so he could get a grant from the Neanderthal Endowment for the Arts. He decided to put two heads on his wall portrait of a woolly mammoth. The critics at the

Endowment hated the drawing, but the caveperson public loved it. And so cartooning was born. While historians have so far been unable to verify this notion, the general point is valid. Humorous drawing is probably as old as drawing itself.

We think there's still a good deal to be learned from artists through the ages who have used drawing for humorous effect. So our examples

Top left: Egyptian comic art; Immediate left: Roman caricature; Above: Leonardo da Vinci; Below: Attributed to Toba Sōjō (Japanese, A.D. 1503–1140)

will come not only from our own work, but anywhere from ancient Egypt and classical Greece to the wonderful twelfth-century animal drawings attributed to the Japanese monk Toba Sōjō and on up to such relatively recent masters of comic visual art as Thomas Hogarth, Honoré-Victorin Daumier, Sir John Tenniel, and Thomas Nast. For it's clear that most humorous artists in any era—whether they were creative cavepersons or contemporary cartoonists, social satirists or political propagandists, representational realists or fabulous fantasists—have used many of the same techniques to get a laugh from their readers. And, though we can't get inside the heads of our predecessors, we suspect they used many of the same methods to generate humorous ideas.

And that's what this book is really about: generating and developing funny ideas.

I
Generating Funny Ideas: Basic Techniques

2
Association: The Key to Generating Ideas

Anyone who does artistic work, be it novel writing, cartooning, or subway graffiti painting, eventually (and then frequently) gets asked, "Where do you get your ideas?" Faced with the question, many artists are likely either to retreat into sullen silence or to be flip:

"There's this little shop in a basement down on Spruce Street. . . ."

"I add a few chopped scallions, a sprig of parsley, a pinch of thyme, and a little cayenne, then stir vigorously over a high flame. . . ."

"Personally, I'd be glad to tell you. But my coven won't let me."

Probably most of us have occasionally wished we knew about a little shop that sells ideas or a cookbook that generates them or perhaps even a coven that helps us create them. At the deepest level, the sources of any artistic idea are a mystery. But simply because there is a mystery involved doesn't mean that we can't understand something about the process of creation. After all, there is a mystery too about the source of a major-league baseball player's idea that he should swing at a fast ball or a singer's idea that she should add such and such a harmony to make the sound exactly right. Yet as anyone who has listened to ball players' endless talk about hitting or singers' endless talk about music knows, neither hitters nor singers believe their ideas are so mysterious that they can't be usefully discussed. Someone born with better reflexes than the rest of us doesn't automatically become a big leaguer, and someone born with a better ear doesn't automatically become a singing star. Good hitters train their reflexes and good singers train their ears. Training—talking about,

9

experimenting with, coming to understand part of the mystery—is what makes the difference between someone with a basic ability and someone with a skill.

In the first two sections of this book we're going to talk about the mystery of getting cartoon ideas.

Let's start with an example. At a cocktail party, one of us was cornered by an eager cartoon fan.

"Show me how you get an idea for a cartoon!" the fan said.

"All right," the one of us said, seized with a mood of careless bravado. "Give me a starting place— any starting place—and I'll come up with a cartoon idea. Then I'll show you how I got it."

The fan looked the one of us squarely in the eye—and noticed that his eyeglasses were held together by sticky tape.

"Your glasses are cracked," the fan said. "Start there."

After about a full minute of dead silence (this assignment is a great conversation stopper), the one of us came up with the following cartoon concept: a long-bearded Jehovah type stands on a cloud above the Earth. The planet is splitting apart as a huge mushroom-shaped atomic cloud billows out from its center. The Jehovah type says to an angel, "Well, back to the old drawing board."

The idea turned out to be too mordant to be salable. (Goya might have done it, had he been a contemporary cartoonist.) But its creation is a good place to begin to talk about how we get our ideas.

The thought process that led from the cracked glasses to the cartoon, as far as the one of us could reconstruct it, went something like this:

Your eyeglasses are cracked. So have them fixed, you nincompoop! Not the point here. But still a good idea. Tomorrow. Too busy tomorrow. Maybe Thursday . . . Get your mind back on the gag! OK, what's funny about cracked eyeglasses? Very little. If I do get them fixed, it'll cost me a mint. Is my MasterCard account up-to-date? Stay on track, idiot! Try this: what *looks* like eyeglasses? A better line of thought. Binoculars look something like glasses. Who looks through binoculars? Bird-watchers. Not interesting at the moment. No help there. What else resembles glasses? Goggles look like glasses. Goggles are funny-looking. A good start.

Should I change the frames while I'm at it? Maybe brown instead of black, with . . . Goggles, remember? *Goggles*! Right. Goggles. Who wears goggles? Swimmers. Snorkelers. Underwater divers. A mental picture of a deep sea diver. Divers could be funny, but how? No help there. Old-time airplane pilots wore goggles. Snoopy, Charles Schultz's dog character, wears goggles. A mental picture of Snoopy atop his doghouse, wearing his aviator's helmet, long scarf, and goggles. That's funny. Why does Snoopy wear goggles? In his fantasy life, he imagines he's flying in a war.

What war? World War I. Not much funny there. What followed World War I? Flappers. Bathtub gin. Who would play gin (rummy) in a bathtub? That's a bit funny, but what could you do with it in a cartoon? Dead end. What came after bathtub gin?

World War II. An image of what was probably the most famous cartoon to emerge from that very unfunny war. Peter Arno drew it. An engineer carrying blueprints for an airplane views a crashed plane. He says, "Well, back to the old drawing board." A proven funny line. Stay with World War II.

What happened during World War II? A series of images: Nazi swastikas; D-Day invasion; raising the flag on Iwo Jima. Not funny. How did World War II end? With the atomic bomb. Not funny either, but the mushroom-shaped cloud is a vivid visual image. A memory of the TV movie *The Day After*, about nuclear holocaust. Frightening. What if it really happened? Who would be around to know? Not people. An image: a standard cliché cartoon picture of a long-bearded Jehovah type standing on a cloud (sometimes he's shown throwing thunderbolts). He'd still be around. Use that. What would he say? Another image of Peter Arno's cartoon, with its caption. And: Jehovah type on cloud, as atomic explosion destroys Earth: "Well, back to the old drawing board."

Note several things about the thinking process here:
First, it was not logical. Thoughts did not move from one idea to

another in the orderly way they would in, say, a lawyer's brief or a philosopher's argument. They moved backward, forward, sideways, from one subject to another, from one time to another, from one place to another, from one medium to another. Perhaps, as some psychologists assert, our minds, left to their own devices, always work in this kind of Alice-in-Wonderland, disconnected way. Minds are, after all, messy receptacles for all kinds of images, beliefs, memories, impressions. It's easy to jump from one set to another.

The method of the jump here was not logic, but *association*. And association is the essence of creating humor. It is also the essence of much other creative thinking. So all who enter the humor business must, at least temporarily, abandon logic. Actually, this fact is one of the delights of the trade. How many fields do you know where you're *encouraged* to stop thinking logically?

Second, there was a good deal of "static" in the associations: thoughts about whether to get the eyeglasses fixed, about what that might cost, about what kind of frames to get. Probably there was even more static than the one of us actually remembered. In subsequent discussions, we'll omit much of the static so we can concentrate on the parts of the association that yield results. But it's well to remember that, even with increased experience, which helps one to focus association in a creative way, some static is always part of the process.

Third, a wide range of ideas appeared in the associations. Probably there were even more than the one of us remembers. Because we're writing a book, we had to put the ideas in sentence form, but most of them certainly did not appear in complete sentences. Many were not even words. There were purely visual images—goggles in various settings, Snoopy, the swastikas, the flag on Iwo Jima, the mushroom-shaped cloud. There were verbal associations—from bathtub gin to playing gin in a bathtub. There was specific material drawn from previous visual artists— the Peter Arno cartoon. And there was material drawn generically from standard cartoon premises—the long-bearded Jehovah, a cliché character in cartooning.

Fourth, the association skipped many steps that would be part of a more orderly thought process. World War II, for example, did not come hard on the heels of flappers and bathtub gin. The Great Depression came in between.

Fifth, the association led to any number of dead-ends like binoculars and bird-watchers and the bathtub gin notion. In a different sequence of thought, these might be the germs of successful ideas. Every set of associations flows differently.

Last, the final, successful production of an idea, came from *combining* associations (the mushroom-shaped cloud and the Peter Arno caption) in a new and unusual way.

All of these comments rightly suggest a disorderly chain of thought. But the process of association here is not quite random. It is, in fact, both free *and* disciplined. For, unlike our normal disorderly mental state and its random sets of images, words, and memories, all of the thinking here was directed toward an end. We were looking for something specific: a funny idea.

We sometimes think of this free but disciplined association process with a homely analogy from fishing. It's like trolling in your mind.

To be successful, you must know where to drop your line in the first place. Then you have to know when to give a jerk to see if you've got something on the other end. Often there will be nothing there, and you'll have to go back to trolling. Furthermore, what you finally pull up may not be a real, live, wriggling whopper of an idea but a spare tire or a piece of seaweed from a cluttered lake bottom. In the example, we came up with a finished cartoon idea, but that doesn't always happen. Here, however, the fishing analogy ends. For when one trolls for funny ideas, it's often possible to take a spare tire or a piece of seaweed and mold, shape, push, punch, and distort it until it becomes a real, live, wriggling whopper.

Everyone who creates visual humor has his or her individual style for getting the process of association going. We know some artists who let their fingers do the walking. They simply sit down with pen in hand, start to draw, and then look at the picture to start associations that may produce a funny caption to go with it or a different funny picture. On the other hand, an artist we know who has been in the business for more than half a century uses a technique akin to that used by the country preachers one of us grew up with. Caught without a sermon prepared, these preachers would open the Bible at random, close their eyes, put a finger down on a verse, and then preach from it. This cartoonist does the same thing with a dictionary. He opens it, closes his eyes, puts his finger on a word, and then builds not a sermon—though there's probably a little of the preacher in all of us in the business—but a cartoon from the associations that flow from that single word.

Still other visual humorists use more ritualized methods. Some work almost exclusively off other people's visual humor. They start with an extant cartoon and see how many associations it engenders or how many variations they can ring on the theme or the caption or the picture. We'll say more about this process, called "switching," in a later chapter. Some work from formalized mnemonic devices. There are, for example, so-called gag wheels and, we understand, even computer programs that list premises for funny ideas: people, props, settings. The artist spins the wheel, takes the combination that appears—say Little Red Riding Hood, an umbrella, and an adult bookstore or an insurance salesman, a broken-down automobile, and a desert island—and tries to move on from there.

As the example about the broken glasses shows, theoretically any-place can work as a starting point. Many artists use a variety of alternative

starting points. But in practice most people find that some starting points work better for them than others. We're going to suggest many starting points, and illustrate how each one works. Experience will teach you which ones will work best for you.

3
Simple Association: Incongruity

A basic element in much—though by no means all—humor is incongruity: the perception of inconsistency between two things. Not all incongruity is funny, of course. As we began writing this book, each of us, separately, received a speeding ticket. The cost was $10 per mile over the recognized speed limit, which made the total for each ticket more than $100. It seemed to both of us that $10 per mile was an incongruously high rate for speeding. But while the cops who gave the tickets may have chortled all the way back to their respective barracks, neither of us got as much as a snicker out of the incongruity. Still, many incongruities *are* funny, or at least contain a germ of a humorous idea. An elementary way to begin to move your mind out from its conventional trolling places into waters richer with funny associations is simply to think about incongruity.

The most obvious incongruities are those that come from the pairing of opposites. Thinking about opposites is one of the most durable and widely used of associative techniques. Virtually every humorist relies on it at some point.

Let's begin with a set of paired opposites we're probably aware of almost from birth: big and small. Historically, this juxtaposition has produced rich veins of humor. Many of the laughs in *Alice's Adventures in Wonderland*, for example, come from contrasts in size. Poor Alice starts by shrinking so that she is only ten inches tall. Next she grows so she bumps her head on the ceiling. And then she shrinks again. Alice is

15

perhaps the most famous use of big and small in humor, but the premise can be applied to an almost endless set of objects and creatures.

Take doors. Doors are an illustration of one technique of association that we'll explore at length later on: the use of props to stimulate funny ideas. But here let's just think about the *size* of doors. They come in all dimensions. There are tiny doors on dollhouses, slightly larger doors designed to let animals (like cats) go in and out of human houses, "regular"-sized doors for humans, bigger garage doors for cars, gigantic doors in public buildings. A good general rule when contrasting opposites is to take the most extreme cases. So what's the largest door imaginable? Arguably it is the door leading into a castle. Visualize a castle. It has a moat around it, and a huge door that, when it's opened, forms a bridge over the moat. There's the *big*.

Now the small. What's little that could come out of our big castle door? A pint-sized creature. How about a flea? A funny idea. Has the flea just bitten the king? Those enormous robes ancient kings wore must have been a penthouse for fleas. Perhaps a flea wonders, "Is there intelligent life on other kings?" But a flea is too tiny to draw effectively against a big door. A slightly larger creature, like a mouse, might work. Is there anything funny about a mouse coming out of a castle door? Possibly, but nothing comes immediately to mind. How about a cat? Now there's a potentially funny idea. Suppose we have the cat come out of the castle. The massive door opens, but only for the small, mundane purpose of letting the cat out at night. The notion is incongruous in a funny way. And we have the cartoon on the facing page.

Note something about the drawing, however. The humor comes not

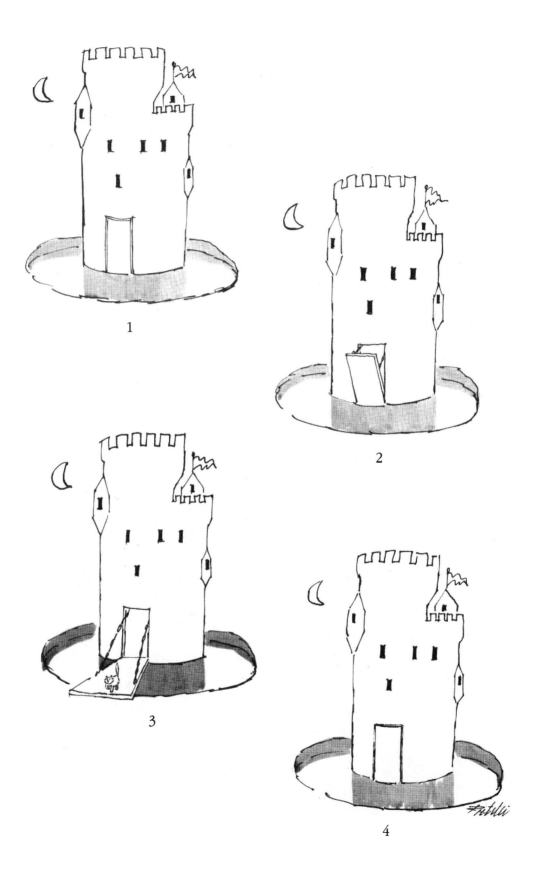

1

2

3

4

so much from the contrast between the massive door and the small
creature making its exit. The humor comes from the massive *effort* it takes
to open the door for such a small purpose. Instead of a single panel
drawing of a cat emerging from the castle, which is incongruous but not
particularly funny, we have a multipanel drawing that illustrates the
cumbersome process of opening the door. The *small* figure of the cat
crossing the bridge is funnier because it comes as a surprise at the end of
the observably *big* amount of work it takes to get the door open.

Suppose we consider another big door, the kind of elaborate, over-
decorated wooden structure that is perhaps an entrance to a room *inside*
the castle. Imagine that door. How would we get it to open? If a door is
not our own, we usually knock. But there is something incongruous about
a small, ordinary knock on such a big door. Take that incongruity, and put
it together with our normal, banal responses when someone knocks at the

"See who's at the door."

door. What do we say? "Come in!" is one response. That might work as a funny line in a movie, where the massive door takes forever to open. The premise can't be made to work quickly enough for a cartoon. What about "See who's at the door"? And we have the cartoon on the opposite page. The huge door makes the small, banal response funny.

As a final example with doors, let's go further afield. We'll take phrases that are associated with doors and see whether they can be applied to doors of different sizes. There are many such phrases. "Knock, knock, who's there?" (Who *is* behind that elaborate castle door?) "Knock and it shall be opened unto you." (Maybe it's a monster or a vampire.) "Opportunity only knocks once." (But kids selling stale candy to earn college scholarships knock again and again and again.) "Build a better mousetrap and the world will beat a path to your door." (What if the creatures behind the door are mice?) Any of these associations could lead to a funny caption. But what's the *shortest* phrase—remember the seven-second rule—associated with doors? It's probably Sinbad's magic formula for opening the door to the treasures the bandits have stored, "Open, Sesame."

Keeping "Open, Sesame" in mind, let's return to big and small doors. We're likely to imagine that the door Sinbad opens with these words is as huge as the castle door and as elaborate as the door to the inside castle room. Suppose, however, we visualize it as smaller, say, the size of the door a cat might use to get into a house. Sinbad can't enter then. But again imagine the huge door. Small cat doors are often built into regular-sized human doors. What if we have a Sinbad-sized door built into a massive portal like the one we imagine? The result is the cartoon above.

Doors are only one small example—with big possibilities—of the juxtaposition of big and small. People can be big and small. Think of Mutt and Jeff, Laurel and Hardy, Abbott and Costello, David and Goliath, Jack (of the Beanstalk) and the Giant, Jack Sprat and his wife. Animals can be big and small. Put an elephant and a mouse together. Or a lion and a mouse. Try a giraffe and a hedgehog. Or, within one species, imagine a St. Bernard and a Chihuahua. There are big and small trees. Try a giant red- wood with a bonsai. There are big and small containers. A saucer can be a bathtub for a sparrow. There are big and small forms of trans- portation. How about putting children's bicycle training wheels on a space shuttle? Or put the wheels on a gigantic yacht. Someone says to the owner of the yacht, "Your first yacht, I presume?"

Big and small, of course, are not only physical characteristics. We use the words as metaphors for other things as well. Take crime and punishment. In one sense, our speeding tickets are an example of this incongruity: the fine was too big for so small an offense (we thought). There are many other big/small incon- gruities in crime and punishment. Some, like the story in *Les Misérables* about Jean Valjean's sentence of many years in prison for the crime of stealing a loaf of bread, induce only anger or pity. But many also induce laughter.

Our lives are fraught with small rules, violations of which generally produce small—or no—consequences. But what if that weren't true? What if the violation of a small rule had incongruously big consequences? Did you ever wonder what would happen to you if you tore off the little tag on a mattress that says "Do not remove under penalty of law?" Imagine a huge punishment for that tiny infraction. Put a character in a prison cell. He says to his cellmate, "Ten to twenty for removing the little tag from a mattress. What'd they get you for?" Or take the incongruity between the small jail sentences often given to people who commit white-collar crimes and the magnitude of their offenses. A judge sentences a defendant who wears a three-piece suit: "Guilty of sending hundreds of thriving busi- nesses into bankruptcy, driving thousands of people out of their jobs, stealing from millions of unsuspecting investors, and bilking uncountable numbers of widows and orphans. Two years, suspended, and 150 hours of community service."

What about disproportionate punishment in other situations? Which of us has not felt unduly punished in a personal relationship for some infraction that we thought small and the other person took as monumen- tal? Picture a domestic scene. One spouse holds a smoking gun over the corpse of the other. What was the dead spouse's small offense? "I warned her not to tell that joke about the elephant and the mouse again." "I warned him not to put his underwear in the hamper with the labels on the outside." Or use the office. There is that infuriating door marked "Authorized Personnel Only." What's our punishment if we open it? Think about a two-panel cartoon. A man opens the door marked "Authorized Personnel Only." What happens? Maybe a devil is on the other side of the door and says, "Finally got you." The boss appears and says "Well, Perkins, there goes your entire pension."

Thousands of funny drawings have come from the big/small contrast. And it is only one on a big list of such contrasts. Ancient versus modern is the source of most historical gags, particularly caveperson gags. It is also the source of one of the most wonderful oxymorons in the current vocabulary of advertising: the notion of a "modern classic." Thomas Rowlandson, the great eighteenth-century British humorous illustrator, took another contrast—chaste versus lecherous—and used it in the drawing shown here to poke fun at a familiar butt of eighteenth-century humor: the ostensibly chaste clergyman who is really a lecher. The drawing is also an example of another technique we'll discuss later: the play on words.

"The Man of Feeling"—
Thomas Rowlandson

Fast versus slow applies to many situations and for some reason works particularly well with animals. Again, when looking at contrasts, the extreme cases are the most useful. The ancient tale about the race between the fast hare and the slow tortoise has spawned endless funny drawings. Similarly, the contrast between in and out has generated endless variations on the letter box premise. Try fat versus thin, free versus chained, neat versus sloppy (the TV show based on Neil Simon's *The Odd Couple* used that premise for years), high versus low, up versus down,

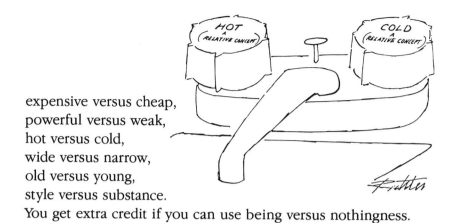

expensive versus cheap,
powerful versus weak,
hot versus cold,
wide versus narrow,
old versus young,
style versus substance.
You get extra credit if you can use being versus nothingness.

A special form of using opposites in cartoons and other humor is the technique called the "reverse." Take an ordinary situation and invert it to make it into its opposite. Consider, for example, a goldfish in a bowl. Goldfish in bowls always contain a germ of humor. A Freudian interpretation might suggest that we fear such containment and so want to laugh at it to relieve the fear. Who puts goldfish in bowls? People. Reverse the situation, put the person in the bowl, and you have the cartoon here. Similar reverses can be wrung from many situations. A horse may have a "people's shoe" hung over its door for good luck, or a rabbit may carry a "people's foot" (grisly, but funny, that). A monkey might laugh at a man who peels a banana. A dog might lead his master on a leash.

There are many ways to find additional opposites. Often simply looking at something and thinking about it suggests them. A coffee mug sits on a desk. The coffee is liquid. What's solid? The coffee is black. What's white? The mug is round. What's square or oblong? The coffee is hot. What's cold? The coffee is wet. What's dry? The mug is hard. What's soft? The mug is shiny. What's dull? A dictionary of synonyms and antonyms can provide more opposites. Some cartoonists jot down pairs as they think of them, and then refer to the list for stimulation when they begin the process of associating for funny ideas. Wherever one finds the opposites, the associations come.

Or—the opposite—they don't. Which leads to our next topic . . .

4
Simple Association: Congruity

Looking for similarities between ostensibly unrelated objects or creatures is the flip side of looking for opposites. The search for similarities can provide an equally good starting point for associations.

A lot of purely verbal humor turns on unexpected and ridiculous similarities. "What's purple and conquered the world?" a seven-year-old asks. "Alexander the Grape!" The humor, of course, comes from the linguistic similarity in the sound of *grape* and *great*. The riddles that cracked us up when we were small may now elicit only a reluctant smile when told to us by someone currently small. But a good deal of adult humor, particularly sexual humor, also turns on puns, double entendres, and other verbal similarities.

A humorous illustrator, however, has a much wider range of similarities to draw from than does a purely verbal humorist. Similarities that engender laughter *can* be verbal in cartoons. There is a whole subgenre of cartoons, including at least one widely circulated comic strip, that relies heavily on verbal similarities in the form of puns. But the cartoonist can also—and generally much more effectively—rely on *visual* similarities. Or, in the best of cases, the visual humorist can create drawings that employ both visual and verbal similarities.

This form of association, then, begins by our asking not "What's the opposite of such and such?" but "What's the *same* as such and such?" There are, however, similarities and similarities, or perhaps similarities within similarities.

Obviously the simplest form of similarity is identity: two objects that are the same. (For this discussion, we'll forget the philosopher's quibble about whether two of anything can be *exactly* the same.) While there is something slightly unusual about pairs that are identical, simply putting two objects or creatures that are exactly the same in one picture will not, as a rule, engender a laugh. But humor can be drawn from people's reactions to the two objects.

The drawing shown here, created over a century and a half ago by the nineteenth-century French caricaturist Honoré-Victorin Daumier, illustrates the apparently universal phenomenon of two people (usually drawn as women, though we suspect more and more men are subject to the same phenomenon) who are irked to discover that they are wearing the same item of clothing. A modern variant is the picture here of a woman and a horse.

Put two identical *people* in the same picture. Again, that is not in itself funny, but the addition of a caption can make the juxtaposition ludicrous.

Honoré-Victorin
Daumier

"I can't keep it from you any longer, Irene.
This is the other woman."

"I'll have whatever he's having."

The first drawing here has an aftertaste: it suggests that we are likely to search continually—and fruitlessly—for the same features in all of the objects of our love. What makes it immediately funny is the banal line about "the other woman." Similarly, the *New Yorker* cartoon shown here is made funny by the insertion of a different, equally banal, line common to watering holes, "I'll have whatever he's having."

Note that in both cases it is essential to establish that the two people who are identical are not twins. In the first drawing, the situation itself suggests that. In the second drawing, the physical distance between the two men implies that they are strangers. However, twins—which have fascinated humans for centuries—can become the subject of humor, particularly if the twins are well known. Romulus and Remus, the legendary founders of Rome, Castor and Pollux, the twins in Greek mythology who are represented by the constellation and astrological sign Gemini, and Tweedledum and Tweedledee in Lewis Carroll's *Through the Looking-*

Glass all come to mind. Today, one might think about clones. A boss introduces several people, one of whom looks exactly like him: "This is Perkins in Accounting, Brewster in Marketing, and Hennesey in Personnel. And, of course, you know my clone, J. R. Billingsly$_2$."

Richer sources for cartoons are objects or creatures that are apparently different, but are similar in one respect. Take a simple object: a bowl. What does it look like? It's metal or it's ceramic or it's plastic or it's glass. Those qualities may suggest similarities with other objects made of the same material, but such similarities are hard to draw. Shape is a more productive similarity. When inverted, a bowl is round. What else has that shape? A lump on the head. A geodesic dome. The dome on the U.S. Capitol. An igloo. A turtle. A turtle beside an igloo is an incongruous situation, though not one that is in itself funny. Suppose we put words in the turtle's mouth. What if the turtle mistakes the igloo for another turtle? What would it say? Make the turtle a baby turtle looking for its mother, and you have a gag line. The turtle, in a famous cartoon, asks "Mama?" The line could, of course, be reversed, and the igloo could say, "Son?"

Perhaps the funniest similarities are those that make people seem similar to other objects or creatures. Many forms of caricature employ this technique. Consider the drawing here, by Daumier. It is a caricature of France's nineteenth-century "Citizen King," Louis Philippe. Daumier drew the king so that his head looks like a pear. The drawing is funny enough in itself, but it actually involves both a visual and a verbal similarity. In French, to call someone a pear (*une poire*) is to imply that the person is not very smart, that he or she has pearlike pulp between the ears. "Soft in the head," we say in English. The savage depiction here by the American cartoonist Thomas Nast, which pictures New York's infamous nine-teenth-century political boss William Tweed as a vulture, employs the same visual and verbal similarity. We call people who habitually prey on the weak vultures.

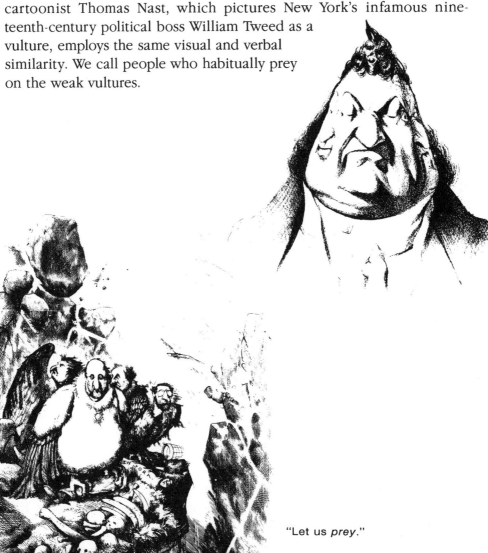

"Let us *prey*."

A whole class of people can sometimes be pilloried by finding a visual similarity. We got to thinking about the way some bosses tyrannize their underlings and wondered how the underlings appear to the boss. He views them as objects, we decided, and probably as objects that can be easily pushed around, even knocked over. We asked ourselves, what is easily knocked over? Bowling pins. The result is the cartoon shown here.

Sometimes, too, one similarity suggests an analogous one. Take the igloo and the turtle cited earlier. What other visual similarities are analogous to the bowl shape these two share? How about a snake and a garden hose, a porcupine and a pincushion, an anteater and a tubular vacuum cleaner with a long nozzle, a rabbit with big ears and a "rabbit-ear" TV antenna, or a seal and a plump human swimmer? The same terse caption—"Mama?"—would work for all.

The point here, of course, is to find similarities between objects that are tangential to our usual ways of thinking and therefore potentially funny. The similarity between a big and a small turtle, or a baby and a Mama snake, for example, is obvious but not funny. The similarity between a turtle and an igloo or a baby snake and a garden hose is.

Some experts on creativity recommend exercises that lead to exactly this kind of unusual association. They suggest that we take any two apparently unrelated objects or creatures—say a banana and a boa constrictor—and ask ourselves how many similarities there are between them. When we tried this exercise with the banana and the boa constrictor, we came up with the following: They both begin with the letter *B*.

Both are longer than they are wide and are therefore at least vaguely phallic. Both grow in tropical climates. Both shed their skins easily. At some stage in their life cycle, both may have a greenish color. We're not arguing that this is the most productive pair of concepts for you to use to begin associations. At the conclusion of this exercise, you may end up only by deciding to call your pet boa constrictor Chiquita. And of course there are also differences between a banana and a boa constrictor, the most significant of which is that banana spelled backwards is *ananab*, whereas boa constrictor spelled backwards is *rotcirtsnoc aob*, or possibly *aob rotcirtsnoc*. But you get the idea.

We've begun with two basic techniques of association: finding differences—particularly in the form of opposites—and finding similarities. We'll employ them in many guises and forms as we move on to discuss more specific kinds of stimulants that can lead to funny ideas.

5
Words as Idea Sources

"Words! Words! Words! I'm so sick of words!" Eliza Doolittle cried in *My Fair Lady*. Poor Eliza. She eventually made it into British high society, but with that attitude she would never have made it as a contemporary cartoonist. For, as we said earlier, one of the qualities that distinguishes cartoonists from most other artists is that cartoonists must be skilled with words as well as pictures. Words, of course, form the basis for captioned cartoons. But words are also a fine starting point for associations that may or may not end up as captioned drawings.

Some words are simply funny in and of themselves. *Curmudgeon* is an intrinsically funny word. Why that's so, we're not sure. Perhaps it's because the word has overtones of pompousness and pretentiousness, and pompousness and pretentiousness are always good targets for humor. Perhaps, too, *curmudgeon* is funny because it contains a hard *k* sound. One theory of humor holds that words that include the hard *k*, like *cupcake, cuckold, cockroach, tickle,* and *fickle,* are inherently funnier than other words.

For whatever reason, a sentence that contains the word *curmudgeon* almost always has a lilt of humor to it and with a bit of work can usually be made overtly funny. A tycoon says to another one, "You're a good curmudgeon, Atwell, but not a great curmudgeon." A pompous husband says to his wife, "Dammit, Martha, I am just being firm. I am not being a curmudgeon." A young woman seduces an older date, "Of course I don't think old curmudgeons are dull, Mr. Balfour." A middle-aged boss with an

31

ample paunch shouts into his intercom, "Miss Dyson, send in a fellow curmudgeon." Or the same boss, now worried, is on the analyst's couch and says, "I think I'm losing the will to be a curmudgeon." Only a curmudgeon could refuse to laugh at those lines.

Other nouns are funny too. Try *grump, gadget, gizmo,* and *geezer* (hilarious if you're not one), or *pickle, poodle,* and *petunia.* Verbs are funny. *Blab, blurt,* and *belch, munch, crunch,* and *scrunch, squish, squash,* and *squabble* are funny verbs. So is *fart.* (It's also a funny noun.) Place-names are funny, at least if you're not from the places they name. Hundreds of verbal gags have been made at the expense of towns like Kalamazoo, Oshkosh, and Padukah. New Jersey is a scream if you're from New York, though we're not sure whether North Dakota is a scream if you're from South Dakota. Animal names are funny. Who can resist a smile over *aardvark, armadillo, bandicoot,* or *hippopotamus?*

Often an intrinsically funny word is a good place to begin associations. But words that have no necessarily funny implications in themselves seem to work equally well. Shakespeare wrote, "A rose by any other name would smell as sweet." But it wouldn't be the same source for associations. Think around roses and you may find rose hips (do roses wear belts above those hips?), "Everything's coming up roses" (a witch complains to another witch about their garden, which is full of flowers, "Dammit, Samantha, everything's coming up roses!"), rose water (do upper-crust roses refuse to drink anything else?), "Lida Rose" from *The Music Man* (which might lead to thinking about barbershop quartets), American Beauty (a rose with inadequate self-esteem complains to another rose, "I'm an American Beauty, but most days I don't feel very beautiful"), thorns (one rose to another: "Dammit, Emily, you knew when you married me I had a thorny personality"), rose beds (one rose seduces another: "Your bed or mine?").

Confusion about words can generate other associations, as in the cartoon here about a befuddled baby duck. Arguments about pronunciations of words can be another source of ideas. Tomatoes are not usually considered to be exactly a laugh a minute. But a moment's thought about how people pronounce the word turned into the cartoon here, used many times by *The New Yorker* in its advertising for subscriptions. Words that are usually associated with others because they are all part of a list are also a good source of ideas. We started with the word *pride,* which actually came from an association beginning with *lions,* as in "a pride of lions." Pride, we remembered, was on the list of Seven Deadly Sins. Suppose, we thought, the judgment about those sins was rendered not at the sound of the proverbial last trumpet, but now, by a jury foreman. The result was this cartoon. (We admit we had to go to a reference book to get

"Mom, are we waterproof or just water-resistant?"

"We find the defendant guilty of pride, covetousness, lust, envy, gluttony, anger, and sloth."

the rest of the words on the list right.) We took a shorter list, the judicial motto of "Truth, justice, equality," and added an additional word to produce this drawing.

Another technique for using words to create funny ideas is one that is sometimes called "comic literalism," that is, taking a figure of speech at its literal meaning. The classic example of comic literalism in verbal humor is the line attributed to Groucho Marx: "When I came to this country, I didn't have a nickel in my pocket. Now I have a nickel in my pocket." But the technique is especially useful in visual humor.

When we write or speak, we use metaphors or similes—words or phrases that imply or state similarities—to spice up ordinary talk and make it more tangy and tantalizing (as this sentence illustrates). Romeo sees a light entering a window and says, "It is the east and Juliet is the sun," and we feel his passion for his lover. A cowboy hero says about another man, "He's a mean sidewinder," and we know the other man is a villain: sneaky and lethal, like a rattlesnake. A friend says, "We've got to stop putting our heads in the sand," and we know she thinks we've been avoiding something unpleasant. A fellow worker, Harrison, returns from his interview with the boss and says sadly, "I guess they're putting me out to pasture," and we know poor Harrison has been moved to some insignificant post or even forced to retire.

All serious subjects, these. Yet if we take any of the above metaphors literally, they are ludicrous. Should Romeo, his skin all red and blotchy above his swimming suit, say, "I guess I stayed too long in the Juliet," we would think him strange—or possibly bawdy—but not passionate. A mental picture of a snake trying to keep a belt weighted with six-guns around its nonexistent waist makes us chuckle. Put the line about "heads in the sand" in the mouth of an ostrich and you get the first picture here. If, as in the second picture here, poor Harrison is actually a horse in human clothing, the sad phrase becomes funny.

"The motion has been made and seconded that we stick our heads in the sand."

"I'm sorry, Harrison, but we're putting you out to pasture."

Perhaps our favorite word sources for cartoon ideas are the jargon words that constantly bombard all of us. "Update," for example, is a jargon word that has, alas, made its way into common parlance. It's pretentious and barbarous, and so good fodder for humor. How many updates on stories have we been forced to view on TV? A man watching TV says, "If I see one more update, I may upchuck." Plug the jargon word into incongruous situations and you have a variety of possible cartoons. A wife may introduce her husband to their kids: "Now, here's Dad, with an update on the family budget." A priest preaches from the pulpit: "Now, an update on sin." A mouse reports to a committee of mice: "Now here's an update from our task force on belling the cat." Or return to the original source of the idea, television, and carry it to its logical extreme. A TV announcer says, "Now here's Dave with an update of Eleanor's update of Bill's update of Ted's update of Margaret's story of last night."

As another example of jargon, take the practice of adding an additional syllable to perfectly respectable words and so turning them into neologisms. For a time there was a tendency to use the prefix *de-* with an almost endless set of words. Industries were deregulated, institutions were demystified, waste dumps were detoxified, territories were demilitarized,

"Sir, I've been debriefed, deprogrammed, and debugged.
May I go home now?"

until our intelligence was almost destroyed. In the drawing here, we took great delight in debunking one of the institutions most responsible for defacing the language—the Defense Department.

These uses of jargon illustrate one of the salient characteristics of cartoons: their transience. Jargon words come and go faster than little boutiques that sell trendy clothing. Today's rib tickler of a takeoff on a currently popular neologism may tomorrow sound as dated as a parody on "twenty-three skidoo" or "your grandmother's underwear." There are, however, ways to stay current with jargon. It's important to keep a keen ear cocked (can one cock an ear?) as you listen to other people's conversations. And, yes, you should listen to other people's conversations. Most professional humorists—perhaps most professional artists—are shameless eavesdroppers. Perusing any of the newsmagazines or viewing as much television news as you can stomach will provide other constant sources of jargon. You may also want to enlist the help of friends. One of us has an "informant," a cartoon lover but not a cartoonist, who is squirreled away in the recesses of corporate middle management. He supplies us with the latest bromides from the American business community. Whatever your sources for jargon words in general use, it's not a bad idea to jot them down as you come upon them.

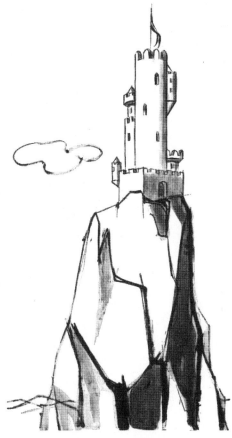

"We're impregnable, dear,
but are we happy?"

You may think you'll recall them, but if you don't put them on paper, you may find yourself de-memoried.

Then, too, you may have access to specialized jargon. Virtually every field generates a set of jargon words. One of us, for example, has spent much of his working life in educational institutions. Among professional educators, jargon words sprout up like so many roses—or thorns—to be harvested by the cartoonist. Words and hyphenated words like *multicultural*, *student-centered*, *hands-on*, *performance-based*, and *curriculum-driven* practically beg to be parodied. We'll talk more later about the creation of cartoons geared to a particular audience. But the workplace is also a fine source of jargon.

Some journalists we know use a game with words to spice up the boredom of routine reporting. Every day someone puts a word or phrase on the newsroom bulletin board—say *impregnable* or *infrastructure* or *catbird seat* or *miasma*. No matter what the assignment, each reporter is supposed to work the day's word into his or her story. That's not a bad way to begin to associate for cartoons.

The good word for today is . . .

"Since you have already been convicted by the media, I imagine we can wrap this up pretty quickly."

6
Clichés as Idea Sources

The next step up, or down, depending on your point of view, from jargon words are jargon phrases—more succinctly, clichés. Ask any teacher of composition to give a set of rules for beginning writers, and high on the list would be "avoid clichés." Clichés are lumps in the smooth sauce of most good writing. But, just as cartoonists often turn reality topsy-turvy in order to get a laugh, so they must often invert the rules of good writing for comic effect. Clichés are essential to cartooning. Remember the seven-second rule. One implication of the rule is that cartoonists, unlike other writers or artists, must deal in premises that a viewer will instantly recognize. That means they must deal with the familiar, even the banal. What is more familiar and banal than a cliché?

Fortunately for cartoonists, if not for those with more refined sensibilities, clichés are all around us. We need only to open our ears (do ears open?) and we're assaulted by them.

Many clichés can be easily translated into cartoon captions. A politician, under fire for some putative transgression, laments, "I've been tried and convicted by the media." What if people really were convicted by the media? A portentous voice from the TV says, "Most observers believe that the collapse of the government in Unztrakyokstan will leave a serious leadership vacuum in the region." What's a leadership vacuum, anyway? The phrase might conjure up a picture of a "leader" vacuum cleaner who directs a pack of voracious "follower" vacuum cleaners as they hungrily forage for dirt. A funny image, that, but perhaps not one that could easily be turned into a full-fledged cartoon. (Then, again, try it.) Back to the metaphor. The collapse of the government in Unztrakyokstan, the TV pundit tries to persuade us, will leave all the folks in that region with a leadership vacuum, that is, with no one to lead them. What will happen to these poor folk? Without leadership, they will presumably all go milling about aimlessly, with no idea of where they should go or what they should do. Just like . . . like what? Like sheep, of course. Suppose there was a leadership vacuum in a flock of sheep. Who would the sheep blame? The answer is in the cartoon here. (Note that the sheep could equally as well have said the line to a shepherd.)

"Speaking frankly, a number of us are worried about a serious leadership vacuum."

The phone rings, and we suspect it's a caller we've been avoiding. We say to our spouse, roommate, or secretary, "Tell them I'm not in." An ordinary situation, a cliché response. But put the line in the mouth of a tycoon in a huge limousine and make the phone a cellular phone, and you get the cartoon here. The line could be transposed to other situations. A king who is surrounded by many court-iers in an elaborate regal setting might utter it as his phone rings. So might an executive at a desk with many tele-phones, all of them ringing simulta-neously. Or the line might be put into the mouth of someone who is receiving a different kind of call, say a Roman emperor in a huge building with an angry mob outside, or a modern-day politician in the same situation. The line can also be said *to* someone un-usual. How about having the family dog about to answer the phone? Or, for that matter, why not have the dog utter the line to its master?

"I'm not in."

"Take no prisoners, dear."

These examples suggest one of the most common—and most effective—ways to use clichés to generate funny ideas. Simply transpose the cliché, which is usually used in one situation, into a different situation. The incongruous situation is what makes the idea work. A fierce warrior, about to go into battle, intones to his troops: "Take no prisoners!" Put the line into the mouth of a wife who sends her husband off to work. Budget-cutters worry about whether programs are cost-effective. The phrase is generally applied to big institutions, like governments and corporations. Apply it to a small institution: marriage. Go even further afield and have the host of a Roman orgy worry about whether the event is cost-effective. People are always talking about "sectors" of the economy—the private sector, the public sector, the manufacturing sector, the service sector, and

"All things considered, I think our marriage has been cost-effective."

"I don't think I've ever met anyone from the Barbarian sector before."

so on. What other sectors might there be? People try to solve their deep-seated psychological problems by joining encounter groups. What if they tried to solve their deep-seated automotive problems the same way?

Sometimes a cliché can be switched into an incongruous situation by changing the character who says it. Often this will involve a slight alteration in the line. Take, for example, the common phrase that a diner looking at a menu might utter to a waiter or waitress: "The filet mignon looks good." Suppose the diner were not human. Let's try an animal—say a cow. The filet mignon certainly would not look good to a cow, unless the cow was a cannibal, which seems a little farfetched even for the world

"You might be interested in our encounter group for people with transmission problems."

of cartooning. What *would* look good to a cow? Hay. Try other animals. A beaver: "The jack pine looks good." A whale: "The plankton looks good." A bee: "The pollen looks good." A vulture: "The carrion looks good." A pig: "The slop looks good." Or try other kinds of nonhumans. A vampire: "The AB negative looks good." An automobile: "The regular unleaded looks good." A computer: "The six-field database looks good."

"The hay looks good."

Verbal clichés are not only good for generating captions. They are also good for generating pictures. Sometimes the transposition from cliché to picture is direct. Take the hoariest of American political clichés, the notion that we are entitled to "life, liberty, and the pursuit of happiness." Hard to achieve in full measure, each of them. Suppose they were as easy to get as, say, aspirin?

"The rich get richer and the poor get poorer," goes the common lament. What if, instead of a reality of economic life, that were the stated purpose of a business?

Substitution, as in the case of the variations on the line "The filet mignon looks good," may also produce pictures. A happy cliché is the one on signs attached to the back of the cars newlyweds drive: "Just Married." Substitutions in the same vein might be "Just Started Living Together," or "Just Divorced." What other events in life might make the participants equally happy? "Just Got Worthless, Lazy Son His First Job," "Just Consolidated Small Debts into One Massive Debt," or (on a car jammed to the gills with junk) "Just Cleaned the Basement for the First Time in Forty Years." These days, particularly for some people in the upper echelons of government, being acquitted might be a happy life event.

Or take the idea of "power" this and "power" that, which in the 1980s became a set of buzzwords (in itself a cliché). Executives were supposed to eat power breakfasts and power lunches, to control power meetings. Where did that leave an executive who liked to take a little snooze after his power lunch? Make a substitution.

POWER NAP

Often a verbal cliché may generate a picture idea in which the cliché is not explicitly stated, but is tacitly understood by the reader. We suspect that such cartoons work particularly well because the reader gets a little extra feeling of "being smart" as he or she mentally supplies the cliché. "He's like a bull in a china shop" turns into an actual bull feeling worried about his transgressions in the shop. If we put the answer to the cliché question, "Which came first, the chicken or the egg?" into the mouth of an actual chicken, we get the second cartoon here. That idea, incidentally, actually combines two clichés: the riddle and the phrase "I shredded the evidence."

"Can you describe this china shop?"

"Just between us, I came first, but I shredded the evidence."

"In a word, gentlemen, we're about to go belly up."

Comic literalism, the technique we mentioned earlier of taking similes and metaphors literally, can make use of cliché phrases as well as individual words for its effect. Business commentators are forever talking about failing companies that "go belly-up." Take the phrase literally and you have this cartoon. Or use the fatuous phrase, "We're all just like one happy family." Make it literal, and you have the cartoon here. Take one of the phrases used to characterize people in the environmentalist move-

"We're just like one big happy family here."

*"Looks as if the clean-air crowd
turned out in force."*

ment, "the clean-air crowd," and ask who that group might literally be. Or, for a more esoteric cliché, use the famous last line of the dying lead character in the opera *I Pagliacci*, "The comedy is finished." That's not funny in itself, but it might be if you put the line in the mouth of the chair of the board of a failing business. What kind of board chair would say the line?

"Gentlemen, la commedia è finita!"

So, instead of avoiding clichés as most good writers do, we urge you to search them out. Read popular journals, watch TV, listen to the way other people talk. Check out a dictionary of slang or a dictionary of clichés. Check your memory. Listen to the way *you* talk. Write down the clichés as you find them. And then tap into an almost limitless source of funny ideas.

For, just between you and us and the lamppost, the clichés we have used here are only the tip of the iceberg, the smallest of fish in a big pond, the glimmer at the end of the tunnel. We urge you from the bottom of our hearts to belly up to the bar and take it from the horse's mouth. From the word go, you should throw caution to the winds, stick your neck out, get a handle on it, get your act together, get into the swing of things, and get up a full head of steam. Then go for broke, go whole hog, go to town, go the route, go haywire, go bonkers, with clichés. Otherwise, when you leap into the fray of cartooning, you'll be up a creek without a paddle, where you'll suffer the slings and arrows of outrageous fortune, piss into the wind, have slim pickings and small beer, probably fall by the wayside, and maybe even give up the ghost, which would be the last straw.

We kid you not.

7
Props as Idea Sources

Imagine you're at the circus. After the heart-stopping antics of the tight-rope walker and the death-defying exploits of the lion tamer, out comes a tiny Volkswagon. A clown emerges from it, then another, then another. Three more clowns appear, another three, yet another three, until at last there are eighteen or twenty. The crowd roars with laughter and applause. What makes the act funny? Partly it is the clowns themselves. We are prepared to laugh at them. But what actually makes the trick work, of course, is the disproportion between the number of clowns and the size of the automobile. The Volkswagon is the real star of the gag.

The Volkswagon is a prop.

Props are standard comic devices for humorous performing artists like clowns. But visual clowns use props no less than their counterparts in the circus. Most props are *visual clichés*. In subsequent chapters, we'll talk about the use of a wide variety of visual clichés in cartooning. Here we'll start with props.

The clowns' use of an automobile for their circus act illustrates a general principle about props that applies to visual artists as well as performing artists. For humor, the best props are also the most common ones. The seven-second rule applies here too. The more familiar the viewer is with the prop, the more quickly he or she will recognize the distortions and incongruities in its use that a cartoonist employs to get a laugh with it.

Earlier we used doors as an example of a prop, but almost any common object can be a starting point for a cartoon. Return for a moment to the circus. One of the clowns who emerges from the VW wears enormous shoes. The shoes get a laugh because they are a disproportionate version of a common item.

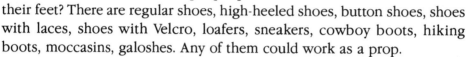

Taking our cue from the clown, we'll start our discussion of props by thinking around shoes. In associating ideas, it's often helpful to think in generic concepts rather than specific ones. So let's not limit ourselves to shoes, but try to think more generally about footwear. What do people put on their feet? There are regular shoes, high-heeled shoes, button shoes, shoes with laces, shoes with Velcro, loafers, sneakers, cowboy boots, hiking boots, moccasins, galoshes. Any of them could work as a prop.

We'll choose galoshes because *galoshes* sounds funny, though anyone who has tried to force a child to wear that kind of footwear knows how unfunny the process can be. Can galoshes be made visually funny? Who

or what might wear galoshes in a way that would be incongruous? Galoshes suggest rain or, more generally, water. We might put them on an aquatic animal, say a hippopotamus. (*Hippopotamus* sounds funny too.) The idea of a hippo who wears galoshes is a little funny in itself. But if we take the memory of a child's reluctance to put on galoshes and combine it with the hippo, we might get a cartoon where a mama hippo insists that her baby wear galoshes before he ventures out into the rain.

What other kinds of footwear are there? Slippers. Dogs go with slippers in a great variety of visual gags. Cinderella wore glass slippers. What might Cinderella's dog do with them, or say about them? What else do people wear on their feet? Ice skates. Thinking about ice skates and using the principle of opposites—roller skates are a kind of opposite—produced this cartoon. Skis are an item of footwear used frequently in cartooning. So are leg casts. How about a foot with a cast on it (perhaps combined with skis)? Ranging further afield with human footwear, we might think about stilts or ten-league boots.

Or think about footwear for animals. We used a hippo in our first example. A famous children's book, *Puss in Boots*, relies on the notion of an animal's wearing footwear for its major premise. Other animals who might wear footwear can also work as premises. Return to the familiar story about the race between the hare and the tortoise. What footwear did they don for the race? And where did they buy it? The ostensibly slow turtle could also put on other kinds of "speedy" footwear: roller skates, a skateboard, shoes with rockets attached to them.

Stay with the idea of an animal buying footwear in a store, and try other creatures. Horses wear shoes. In the same way humans may look at many shoes before they buy, a horse might force an exhausted human salesperson to show an enormous variety of shoes before the animal found a style to its liking. Or take the creature that would have the biggest problem with footwear: a centipede. Centipedes have provided the stimulus for hundreds of feet and footwear gags.

"That's one small step for a flea, one giant step for flea-kind."

(A final example with footwear. When we began this discussion, we intended to stay with the more or less literal use of props, but we couldn't resist one idea that is the result of a *verbal* association with footwear. Our thoughts went from shoes to feet to the steps people take with their feet to perhaps the most famous quotation about steps ever uttered. Then, in keeping with our discussion in the chapter on words about slightly altering spoken lines, we generated this idea.)

It is but a small step from footwear to other items of clothing. Virtually any of them can provide a comic premise. Transposing the common cowboy hat symbols into an incongruous setting produced this *New Yorker* cartoon. A hairsbreadth away from hats are hairdos. A banal

modern phrase plugged into a caveperson situation produced this idea.

Items of furniture also make good props. An American illustrator used a bed as a prop to poke fun at a common butt of humor in the nineteenth century: Mormon polygamy. From a bed, id's only a small step to the reclining device that has probably spawned more cartoons than any other: the analyst's couch. Lamps can be used in many ways. So can tables, desks, chairs, stoves, refrigerators, footstools, and sofas.

"Aren't you wearing your
hair differently?"

"Now just relax, Louis, and tell us all
about yourself."

In Memoriam Brigham Young
"And the Place Which Knew Him Once
Shall Know Him No More."

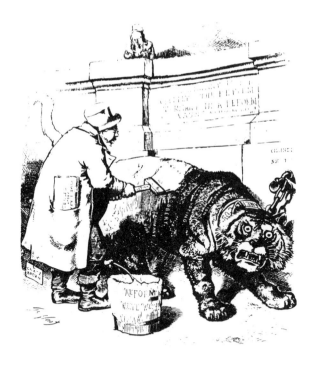

THROWING DOWN THE LADDER BY WHICH THEY ROSE.

Other common household items provide a basis for many humorous drawings. A paintbrush prop makes Thomas Nast's savage cartoon about the "tiger" of Tammany Hall politics particularly effective. In another drawing, Nast used a ladder and a wall—in this case a famous wall, the Great Wall of China—to lampoon America's exclusion of Chinese immigrants. George Cruikshank, the Victorian English visual satirist, got back

at a publisher who had stolen his work by using a common household object of his time: fire tongs.

Let's go even further afield. Instead of thinking *about* a prop, try to think *like* a prop. Of course props are inanimate. They don't really think. Or do they? Maybe somewhere there's a Prop Liberation Movement. Even if there isn't, one of the conceits of cartooning is that we can make just about anything do just about anything. Anthropomorphize an inanimate prop and ask how *it* would feel about a given situation.

Clouds are inanimate. We imagine that their shapes make pictures. But what if a cloud *tried* to make pictures? TV sets are inanimate. Occa-

sionally, though, we think they have a mind of their own. What if one really did? Billiard balls seem to be totally inanimate objects. Suppose they had feelings too?

Chess pieces are inanimate, though they at least represent human figures. In *Through the Looking-Glass*, Lewis Carroll animated them into believable (and, for Alice, infuriating) creatures. We took our lead from Carroll's book to use the most elementary rule of chess and make it into

"Damn it, Gwendolyn, you knew when you married me I only moved one square at a time."

a metaphor for a husband-wife conflict. We could have tried many other inanimate objects. What would a book think about someone who was reading it, a garbage pail about someone who was putting a trash bag into it, a mirror about someone who was looking into it?

All of the above are examples of the use of props in situations where the props stay more or less in their actual form. But props are a fruitful beginning place for more far-ranging associations that employ the rules of similarity.

Return for a moment to the field of humorous performance. This time imagine that you're in a theater. Two mimes, a man and a woman, walk toward one another. Each carries an open umbrella. The umbrellas get tangled up as they pass one another. The pair become irate. The woman folds up her umbrella and attacks the man with it, using it as if it were a sword. The man uses his open umbrella as a shield. The woman accidentally stabs herself in the toe with her umbrella and hops around in pain. As he watches her, the man uses his umbrella as a stool to sit on. He laughs so hard he falls off the stool. The woman laughs.

Still angry, the man and woman stand back to back, like duelists. The umbrellas come up on their shoulders, as if they were rifles. The pair march away from one another, turn, aim the rifles, fire. The woman falls. Stricken with remorse, the man rushes toward her. He opens his umbrella, lays it on the stage with the handle in the air, and scoops imaginary water out of the imaginary basin the umbrella makes. The water revives the woman. The two smile at one another, leap up, and do a soft-shoe dance, using their now-closed umbrellas as canes.

Before our eyes, the simplest of props has been transformed. In rapid order, an umbrella has become a sword, a shield, a stool, a rifle, a water basin, and a cane. In a different routine, the umbrella could be a birdbath, a flagpole, a gigantic phallus, a microphone to croon into, a subway strap to hang on, a hook to pull offending actors offstage.

Cartoonists can make the same transformations. An umbrella cartoon may not spring immediately to mind. But surely there is a cartoon idea in a sword or a shield, a stool or a rifle, a water basin, a cane, a birdbath, a flagpole, a phallus, a microphone, a subway strap, or a hook.

Let an umbrella—or another prop—be your route to a smile on a rainy, rainy day.

8
Settings as Idea Sources: The Home

An obvious but important fact about cartoons is that the humorous situations they depict are almost always shown as taking place somewhere. Cartoons usually have a *setting*.

That's not necessarily true for other forms of humor. Many examples of purely verbal wit, for example, exist in a kind of spatial limbo, with no suggestion of a setting at all. Someone starts a joke: "These two psychiatrists are discussing their patients. One shrink says . . ." *Where* are the psychiatrists? In a medical office? On a street corner? In a subway car? On the moon? It doesn't matter. The joke works perfectly well without a physical location. Other forms of verbal humor demand only the barest minimum of setting. "A guy is sitting in a bar," says a jokester. "An elephant rushes in, orders a martini, gulps it down, then walks up the wall, across the ceiling, down the other wall, and out the door. The guy says to the bartender . . ." We don't need to know anything about what the bar looks like to get the joke.

But a cartoon, because it is a drawing, generally needs a sense of place. Like the best props, the best cartoon settings are those that are most common and therefore most easily recognizable.

Settings play different roles in different kinds of visual humor. There are some cartoons that are akin to placeless verbal jokes. They are basically "talking heads" ideas that rely almost exclusively on a funny caption for their humor. Settings for these gags are neutral, almost irrelevant. For example, *New Yorker* cartoons have historically relied heavily on two settings for such jokes: the cocktail party and the bar. The three cartoons here are examples. Two take place at a cocktail party, one in a bar. But all three could be set in either location. Other examples of more or less neutral settings into which these lines could be inserted are a restaurant, a fancy men's club, or a dinner party.

Note, though, that while the specific settings for these ideas are irrelevant, the drawings are not. A skilled cartoonist will design a visually funny element even for a "talking head" idea. In these cartoons, the visual characterizations of the individuals who speak make the captions work better. We recognize the self-important tycoon who utters the first caption and the fatuous intellectuals who utter the other two captions because of the way they are drawn, and so find the lines even funnier.

While there are such virtually "placeless" cartoons, most cartoons

"But enough about my unique brand of Americanism. Tell me about your unique brand of Americanism."

*"My feeling is that while we should have the deepest respect for
reality, we should not let it control our lives."*

need to be anchored in a specific visual space.* For some cartoons,
settings provide a backdrop, without which the idea would not make
sense. In others, the setting itself may provide a stimulus for an idea. We'll
talk about a variety of settings. Some suggest general topics for cartoons.
Others generate specific ideas associated with a particular place.

---

*All rules have exceptions. The drawing of the irate husband and wife who
glare at each other because one wears ice skates and one roller skates on page
51 works because there is no setting. Any specific setting would make the
cartoon unbelievable.

"Then we've agreed that all the evidence isn't in and even if all the evidence were in, it still wouldn't be definitive."

Probably the most common setting for modern magazine cartoons is the home. Since most of us spend more time at home than anywhere else—except perhaps at work—the domestic setting is rich with familiar comic situations that viewers can easily recognize and with which they will identify. We have found, though, that home settings do not, in and of themselves, provide much stimulus for cartoon ideas. Instead, the settings suggest a range of topics about which ideas can be developed by the use of other associational techniques.

The most widely used premises for cartoons with home settings are those that involve husbands and wives. A good general rule is that a funny idea about domestic couples should—at least implicitly—involve *conflict* between the two.

The nineteenth-century drawing here, by Daumier, illustrates how universal is the appeal of husband-wife conflict for comic art. Although a modern cartoonist might draw the picture with less violent physical action, the situation is one we can all recognize: a spat between husband and wife. Daumier's drawing is funny enough in itself, but it can also be used as a stimulus for a modern cartoon idea. In fact, the picture practically begs for a modern caption. What does she say to him? In Daumier's actual caption, they are arguing about her housekeeping. What else might they fight about? Try one of the other associative techniques we've used. Find a word that might work in a caption here. Or a cliché.

LIZ AND ED ANDERSON
A VERY COMPLEX RELATIONSHIP

Honoré-Victorin Daumier

Take the spat one step further. What happens when it is over? The couple reconcile. Two historical drawings, one by Daumier and one by Rowlandson, again show the universality of the premise. And again, while the pictures are funny enough in themselves, they can be stimuli for modern captions. What is the husband in the Daumier picture saying? Take a cliché: "Dammit, Evelyn, you knew when you married me that . . ." That what? ". . . that I dropped cigar ashes on the rug." ". . . that I was a miserable excuse for a husband." What is the husband by the door in the Rowlandson drawing thinking? What does *he* say?

Honoré-Victorin Daumier

"After the Quarrel"—Thomas Rowlandson

Honoré-Victorin Daumier

Honoré-Victorin Daumier

Instead of using clichés, try to generate a funny line by the principle of opposites. What's supposed to be the basis for a marriage? The mutual passion shown in this drawing of courtship by Daumier. What's the opposite of such mutual passion? The mutual boredom that can come after courtship turns into marriage, shown in the second Daumier drawing. Daumier depicted his scene in the early nineteenth century. In the

early twentieth century, cartoonist Art Young took the same premise and added an animal—a household dog—to emphasize the boredom theme. Our modern updating adds a prop (the TV set) and anthropomorphizes it to make a similar comment. An early nineteenth-century drawing by James Gillray here utilizes a verbal pun to illustrate the "after marriage" premise. All these pictures stem from the same pairing of opposites.

Harmony *before* Marriage
James Gillray

Matrimonial Harmonics
James Gillray

There's another method of association—one we haven't yet discussed—that will work here too. Often we can produce a new set of funny ideas by taking a situation and thinking about it backward or forward in time—by asking "What happened before this?" or "What will happen after this?"

Look at one of our bored married couple pairs. What happens later? A likely modern scenario is that they become so bored with one other that they get divorced. But, as anyone who has participated in or observed the end of a marriage knows, while divorces may be legally final, they are seldom psychologically final. Something of the former partner always lingers in the divorced person's head.

We asked ourselves how we could visually suggest that insight. Our immediate impulse was to take a physical object—a photograph of the ex-spouse, a piece of his or her clothing, perhaps a favorite object—and put it in a drawing as a prop. Then we thought, "What if, in some way, the ex-spouse himself or herself stays around?" The result is this cartoon. The aftertaste of the drawing comes from its statement of the truism about the psychological residues of divorce. The immediate humor comes from a melding of a setting (for the drawing to work, it is best placed in a family room or living room), a prop (the easy chair), a cliché word (*aura*), and visual comic literalism (turning an aura into a physical presence).

"That's Henry's aura. It hung around here after we got the divorce."

Specific areas of the home may also suggest particular subjects for domestic conflict. Think bedrooms and you're likely to think about sex. How much did that have to do with the divorce? Henry's aura does not exactly exude foxiness. Think dens or studies and you may get a range of associations about conflicts between spouses where one is spendthrift and one miserly, or one is messy and one tidy—other sets of opposites. Try the kitchen or dining room. What conflicts might take place there? The Daumier drawing here suggests one. What does he say to her? Use a cliché line: "Look, Françoise, you knew when you married me that at breakfast I kept my nose buried in the goddamn newspaper." Guest bedrooms, laundry rooms, rumpus rooms, bathrooms, garages, or basements can suggest other conflicts.

Various rooms in the house also contain props. Think around garbage pails (who takes out the garbage?), cooking equipment (remember Jack Sprat and his wife), TV sets (do they have one bedroom, but separate televisions?), sofas (remember how many Dagwood jokes are built around that furniture item). Take a mental tour of your own residence and see what the settings and the props suggest. You'll find many new ideas that prove that there's no place like home.

9
Settings as Idea Sources: The Workplace

If the home heads the list of common settings for cartoons, the workplace comes in a close second. Among workplace settings for cartoons, the one most frequently used is the office. Again, familiarity is the key to successful cartooning. Even people whose jobs are located in other situations have encountered enough offices to make the locale easily recognizable in cartoons.

Two observations we made about cartoon ideas set in the home apply equally to those set in the office. We have found that merely thinking about an office, in and of itself, does not generate many funny ideas. Instead, the office suggests a range of topics about which ideas can be developed by the use of other techniques of association. And, as with domestic cartoons, the best office cartoons are those that involve conflict.

The most common source of office conflict—or at least the one that has generated the most cartoons—is the relationship between bosses and employees. Cartoons about that relationship can take the point of view of either the boss or the employee. For certain audiences, a cartoon that takes the boss's perspective and puts the employee in an unfavorable light by depicting him or her as stupid, lazy, or incompetent will work. But since many more people are employees than are bosses, most boss-employee cartoons take the employee's point of view. Curiously, even bosses often find antiboss cartoons funny. After all, the gag applies to other bosses or perhaps to bosses in general, but not—perish the thought—personally to them.

Take the employee's point of view, then. How do employees perceive bosses? Right or wrong, bosses are often viewed as people whose main function is to deny things to employees. That perception is the starting point for many office conflict cartoons. The employee wants something. The boss doesn't want the employee to have it.

Using this premise, we started with a simple word association. What's the most elementary word associated with denial? Obviously, it's simply *No.* To put a boss and an employee together in a picture and have the boss just say "no" is not in itself a funny idea. But suppose—as many of us at least sometimes believe—the boss *always* says no. You could draw a boss who says to an employee, "Whatever it is you want, Perkins, the answer is 'No.'" That might work as a successful caption. We took the idea a step further, and asked what would happen if the boss simultaneously said "no" to *everyone* in the organization. How might he do it? The result is the cartoon here.

"Memo to all departments: No!"

Suppose we have the boss deny the most basic thing any employee wants in a work setting: to keep his or her job. In real life, "You're fired" is one of the least funny lines anyone can hear. But, perhaps because we fear losing our jobs and so want to laugh in relief when the disaster happens to someone else, the firing of employees is one of the most common premises for office gags.

Again, the simple line, "You're fired" won't work on its own. What can be added to it? Does the boss give reasons for getting rid of the employee? If so, the employee will almost certainly think the reasons are arbitrary. Make them arbitrary. The boss says: "Don't take it personally, Hawkins. We're firing all personnel who part their hair in the middle," or "We're firing all personnel who hum show tunes under their breath." As an alternative, have the boss use a jargon phrase to justify the firing. "Don't think of it as being fired, Hawkins. Think of it as being part of the readjustment in the work force necessary to make America competitive in the global economy of the twenty-first century," or "Think of it as Nature's way of thinning the corporate herd." Maybe the boss equivocates slightly when he or she fires the employee. "You're fired, Hawkins. Pending . . ." What? "Pending notification of next of kin." "Pending an environmental impact study." Any of these verbal premises—"Don't take it personally . . . ," "Think of it as . . . ," or "You're fired, pending . . . ," and many others, can be the basis for office cartoon ideas.

Employee-boss cartoons are frequently a way for employees vicariously to get back at the boss, usually by focusing on the boss's foibles. Think of personality characteristics that are frequently attributed to bosses. Vanity is one. Targeting vanity in bosses is an almost surefire way to get a laugh. Two cartoons here, one set in the office, one set in a businessmen's club, use the same premise—the pretentious use of the plural pronoun "we" to describe a single person—to lampoon the self-

"Of course, there's the editorial 'we' and the royal 'we' but I've always felt the corporate 'we' carried the most weight."

important manners of bosses. Perhaps an even more effective use of the theme of vanity is the cartoon here. The drawing was published in the 1940s. A contemporary version would have to employ a more modern depiction of the dictating machine prop, but the basic idea is not dated at all.

"Very amusing, Robertson, if I were the type to be amused."

Another putative quality of bosses—humorlessness—provided the basis for this cartoon. Think of other characteristics often attributed to bosses: indifference to the feelings of employees, money-grubbing, self-promotion, cowardice in dealing with the person next up the line of command, perhaps self-pity for being "lonely at the top." Try them out as the basis for boss-employee ideas.

On your own time, of course.

Conflicts between bosses and employees are paralleled by conflicts between employees. Think around the standard subjects for conflicts between workers in an office: fights over promotions, scrambling for perquisites like office space and office furniture, disagreements over who should do a job, battles over who's doing the most work. Take characteristics of fellow-workers that most people find disagreeable: procrastination, stupidity, avarice, callousness, aggressiveness. Or take office "types" that are recognizable: the nonstop talker, the flirt, the clock-watcher, the shirker, the procrastinator, the go-getter who stomps all over everyone else. Each of them can become the basis for many cartoons.

Conflicts *within* an employee are also a fertile field for funny ideas. A raft of office slogans and posters —"I love my job; it's the work I can't stand," "I live for weekends"—attest to the fact that most of us probably feel a love-hate relationship with our work. It's the hate part of our ambivalent feelings that generates humor. Someone who always loves his or her job is likely to be thought funny as in crazy, not funny as in ha-ha. How do people deal with hating their jobs? They may rationalize. They may imagine that they deserve a better job and believe that only circumstances beyond their control have denied it to them. Thinking about all of the ways in which people deal with their job dissatisfactions is another fruitful source of cartoon ideas.

*"Our recommendation, then, is that we all take
a little under the table."*

Like homes, offices have areas that suggest particular kinds of funny ideas. The posh boardroom, which most employees never see, becomes the locus for many drawings, particularly those that lampoon the pretentiousness or greed of corporate boards. Think about the water cooler and you may think about office gossip, or perhaps about a boss who complains that employees spend too much time there. Think about little cubbyholes in huge rooms and you get images of the rat race. Office events can be turned into humor. Think of payday (when there are more deductions than pay), the farewell dinner, the office party, the committee meeting, the coffee break.

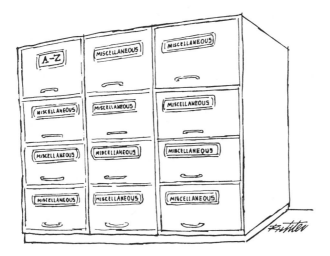

Offices are also full of props that can become the basis for humor. Because all of us are disorganized some of the time and some of us are disorganized all of the time, filing cabinets are a standard prop for office gags. Telephones, the ultimate "you can't live with them and you can't live without them" piece of technology, are another. Take the simple matter of being put on hold. What is more infuriating? Fight back with a cartoon.

The more office technology expands, the more props there are for gags. The growth of complex communication technology means that telephones can do everything from digest computer information to water your lonely office geranium. Think about ancillary office telephone equipment, including answering machines, intercoms, conference call facilities, cellular phones. Computers are a fact of life in virtually every office and an almost endless source for humor. Try photocopy machines,

fax machines, overhead projectors or slide projectors, workstations. Or, if complicated technology becomes overwhelming, think about specific kinds of offices and use the most common of all props: the sign.

Although offices are the most easily recognized workplace, many other job settings can generate gags. A job that involves direct relationships with customers offers a range of comic possibilities, as the many variations on the cliché setting of the Complaints Department attest. The offices of professionals like doctors, dentists, or lawyers are also rich with potential jokes. So are supermarkets, department stores, hospitals, libraries, courtrooms, automobile garages, laboratories, and schools. One word of advice about these settings: the more uncommon the work situation, the more likely it is that the cartoon should be conceived from the consumer's point of view. Few people work in doctor's offices, but many people have visited them. Few of us labor as librarians, but most of us have taken out a book.

If relatively common work situations become boring, let your mind go further afield. Think about the settings for unusual jobs. Try midair (a professional sky diver), a cave (a professional wine taster), the ocean depths (a professional scuba diver), atop a tall pole (a professional trapeze artist), a cage (a professional lion tamer). With each job, think about the setting, about props usually seen in the setting, about words or clichés that are associated with the trade. The U.S. Census lists more than 500 occupational categories, most of which can be subdivided into even more categories. That adds up to thousands of possible workplace situations. Any of them can be legitimate grist for the cartoonist's mill.

There's one exception. Jokes about professional humorists are off-limits. We labor in secret locations best left undescribed. Besides, we take our work very seriously.

10
Settings as Idea Sources: Exotic but Familiar

Paradoxically, some of the settings employed most frequently for cartoons are places that no one has ever seen. Yet when cartoonists use these settings, they still follow the seven-second rule, which demands that the viewer instantly recognize the situation. The explanation of the apparent contradiction is simple. The settings have been depicted so often that we are almost as familiar with them as we are with our own home or office. They are part of the visual furniture of our culture and, therefore, of our minds.

Take Heaven and Hell, for example. We've never met anyone who claims actually to have visited either place. But we all feel familiar with, if not exactly comfortable in, each location. In the Western world, artists have provided both visual and verbal depictions of paradise and punishment in the afterlife since long before the Christian era. With the advent of Christianity—and particularly in the Middle Ages—the two settings became a preoccupation for artists. That great literary prototype for all modern buddy movies—Virgil and Dante's journey in *The Divine Comedy*—is but the best-known example. Most medieval depictions of Heaven and Hell were presumably not intended to provoke laughter. Still, we can't help but imagine that the patrons of Hieronymus Bosch, that wonderful illustrator of afterlife alternatives, found some of his depictions funny. Certainly they evoke a chuckle in a modern viewer.

In any event, modern cartoonists frequently use Heaven and Hell to generate laughter. Both settings can be good stimuli for the creation of cartoon ideas. But it's our experience that these visual cliché settings do not work as stimuli in quite the same way as more real locations. A few of the associative techniques we have mentioned will occasionally work with these locales. Some props and characters go with the settings and can be used to stimulate ideas. Heaven (so we imagine) is full of harps and halos, of men and women who wear long robes and of stern men who wear long beards. Hell is full of fires and pitchforks, of men and women who wear nothing at all, and of stern men who wear long horns. Some words and phrases also go with each setting.

But a more helpful way to use these settings is a method of association we haven't yet mentioned: think about the *states of mind* connected with each locale.

Start with the process of getting into Heaven or Hell. Entry involves

"Well, you were right. Neatness didn't count."

someone judging us. The state of mind judgment evokes is likely to be *guilt.*

Picture the applicant for eternal status standing before the visual cliché most often used in the Heaven and Hell premise: St. Peter at the Pearly Gates holding the Big Book of Life. What does the applicant feel guilty about? Did he or she once refuse to put on galoshes, and so make Mom unhappy? Once tear the little tag off a mattress? Once walk through a door marked Authorized Personnel without being authorized? Once keep a library book for years and years? Once—or more than once—cheat on I.R.S. form 1040? In a cartoon, St. Peter might find any of these offenses relevant to the applicant's status.

The applicant may provide justification for entry into Heaven with a recitation of equally trivial good points about his or her life before this important moment. "I always put my underwear in the laundry hamper right-side out." "I never once missed a payment on my MasterCard." "I always remembered my Mom's birthday." "I never once used the office phone for personal calls." The basic humor technique in all of these gags, of course, is the contrast between the opposites big and small: a big—in this case enormous—judgment that might hinge on very small items of behavior.

Assuming the applicant is assigned to one place or the other, additional states of mind can be invoked to generate funny ideas. Heaven, for example, can be a metaphor for yearning. What do we want that we might get in Heaven, which would make it a true paradise? Is the happy hereafter an eternal table set with delicious but no-calorie and no-cholesterol food, a fishing spot where they're always biting, a theater where we always get the starring role, a bowling alley where we consistently score 300, a stock exchange where prices on our stocks only go up, a committee meeting where we forever get our way? Or—on a more mordant note—is it a place where we have endless opportunities successfully to get back at our enemies?

Heaven may also evoke nostalgia and regret. We're told we can't take it with us. If we can't, what might we miss that we couldn't? A lawyer might miss her litigation, a tycoon his sycophantic underlings, a queen her courtiers, a sports buff the Super Bowl, a gambler the regular Saturday night poker games. Or picture someone who could and did take some of it with him or her. What would we most like to take? Money? Our favorite teddy bear? The car we just finished paying for? Inserting props not usually associated with Heaven into a picture can generate many ideas.

If Heaven evokes yearning or nostalgia, Hell is likely to generate feelings about those things we fear. What are the worst parts of our lives? Perhaps Hell is a place where *all* food is high in calories and cholesterol, a fishing spot where nothing ever bites, a theater where we're always upstaged, a bowling alley where the pins are cemented to the floor, a stock exchange where prices on our stocks always go down (or, even more diabolical, where we never know whether they're going up or down), an endless committee meeting where nothing ever gets decided.

Perhaps in Hell we are only allowed to take with us the worst parts of our life. We argue many court cases, but never win. Our yes-men just say no. Our courtiers refuse to bow and scrape. The Super Bowl never happens or we never learn the score. We always lose the poker game. All our money turns out to be from a Monopoly set. Our favorite teddy bear hates us and runs off with another human being. We can't keep the car with us, but we still have to make the payments.

"But they don't say plus or minus, you'll notice. You can't get more fiendish than that."

"I just barely made it."

If Heaven and Hell are places no one we know has ever seen, other cliché cartoon settings are perfectly real, but so exotic that few of us have ever laid eyes on them. Yet visual depictions of these settings—whether in television programs and movies or in fine art—have made them familiar enough that they too generate feelings in us.

Most of us have never been inside a prison, for example, but images of prisons evoke some of the same fears about punishment—and the same rationalizations—as images of Hell. Prisons also evoke fears of confinement. Almost no one nowadays has been a party to a duel, but the cliché setting of a field at sunrise evokes feelings about conflict. No one has ever been on another planet and only a handful of people have even walked on the moon, but settings on weird-looking planets or in outer space may evoke feelings of wonder about the universe and of curiosity about what creatures may exist beyond our ken, or they may become ways to reflect on the foibles of humankind.

Places like prisons and outer space begin to shade into another category of visual cliché locales. These are settings that are easily recognized not so much because they are frequently depicted in the culture at large as because they are frequently depicted by cartoonists. They are, in a sense, internal clichés to the field of cartooning.

The hoariest of cliché cartoon settings—the desert island, with a person or people marooned on it—is a good example. The theme of a shipwreck that leaves a traveler miserable or washes him or her up on some strange shore is ancient. It has been used in works as diverse as

"Misery"—Thomas Rowlandson

Homer's *Odyssey*, Shakespeare's *Twelfth Night*, and Defoe's *Robinson Crusoe*. In these days of air travel, though, fewer and fewer people have actually been on a ship, let alone experienced a shipwreck. Yet the image of the castaway on the island is still powerful.

The desert island image affects us powerfully because it is a metaphor for loneliness. We are both fascinated by and afraid of what might happen to us if we were, like the castaway, left alone for a long time. Assume the castaway is male. What does he do to assuage his loneliness (what might we do to assuage our loneliness)? He wants someone to talk to. Who? A common prop in desert island cartoons is a single palm tree. Does the castaway befriend the palm tree, carry on long, intimate conversations with it, fall in love with it, have a lover's quarrel with it and refuse to say a word, berate it as though it were his spouse, fantasize that it's his Mom, imagine it's his boss?

By talking to the tree, our castaway is trying—as any of us might—to re-create normal "civilized" life in the face of terrible isolation. How else might he do that? Ever hopeful, he erects a mailbox on his desert island. Nostalgic for familiar things, he puts up a needlepoint sampler: "Desert Island, Sweet Desert Island." Insert modern props. There is a television set. It shows only a picture of a desert island. The palm tree answers a telephone. The castaway says "I'm not in." Or perhaps the castaway is a tycoon who has been exiled to the island for some reason and re-creates his old setting.

ARBITRAGEUR IN EXILE

"Of course, you understand that you can't possibly
stay here tonight."

On the other hand, we may view the desert island as a chance to escape from some aspects of civilization that we don't like. The humor then comes from the feeling that we are trapped, that civilization is an omnipresent—and oppressive—force that we carry with us as a part of our mental baggage. We can externalize that notion in a cartoon. Somehow the banal, the everyday, creeps onto our island paradise. The castaway crawls up onto the island and finds—what?—a "No Smoking" sign, an I.R.S. agent, a billboard, a fast-food restaurant. Another common prop for desert island cartoons is a bottle that has floated up from the sea and contains a message. What's the message? A reminder from our dentist that we missed our regular six-month checkup? Our MasterCard bill? A request for a donation from our alma mater? An advertisement for a contest, first prize being a trip to a remote, exotic island?

Put two people on the desert island, and you evoke the fear we all have of being confined to just one human relationship. As they arrive, they carry conventional attitudes into this unconventional situation. If the pair has been alone on the island long enough, presumably each has heard all of the other's jokes, listened to the other's complete life story, learned all of the other's small, irritating quirks.

It's but a small distance for a cartoonist from a desert island to yet

"Junk food! Junk food!"

another cliché setting: the desert, with a parched, bedraggled man on his hands and knees—a "desert crawler" in the parlance of some cartoonists—who makes his way across the dunes. We don't know anyone who actually had this experience and lived to tell the tale. But as a metaphor, the desert crawler is wonderful. The ruling feelings in crawler cartoons are deprivation and desire.

What does the poor man want? "Water! Water!" is the standard line. What else? Start with other drinks—"Dry white wine with a slightly fruity nose!" "A mixture of orange juice and pineapple juice with just a dash of cranberry to add zest!" Move to food—"High fibre, low-fat cuisine!" "An ecologically sound source of protein!" And then move on to almost any other subject—"Honest politicians!" "Better daytime television!" "An

economic panacea!" Add another cliché element to the scene—a mirage— and the ruling feelings become hope and delusion. What does the crawler see? In the traditional picture, an oasis appears. The range of other things that might appear is limited only by the cartoonist's imagination.

Cliché cartoon settings need not be so farfetched as the deserted

island or the desert. A quick perusal of cartoons in a few magazines will generate many other such settings. None are common in actual experience. But each is easily recognizable to a cartoon viewer, and each evokes a particular set of feelings: the editor reading an author's manuscript (fear of rejection), the lawyer's office with the heirs present (greed, perhaps disappointment), "Mom's Diner" (desire for parental approval, fear of parental reprimands), parks with unusual statues (pretentiousness, self-importance, how about combining a statue with Mom?), the courtroom bailiff swearing in a witness (fear of lying).

Although some editors claim that premises like these have been overdone and should be avoided, our experience is that an original idea can be generated out of any of them. The emotions they evoke are universal. The challenge is not so much to see the setting in an original way as it is to feel the emotions in an original way.

11
Characters as Idea Sources

Recall a particularly striking novel, play, or movie. Chances are the first aspect of it that comes to mind are the characters: Scrooge or Scarlett O'Hara, Macbeth or Mickey Mouse, Charlotte the Spider or Conan the Barbarian. Novelists, playwrights, and filmmakers spend much of their time creating—or, many of them would say, discovering—the people in their works of fiction.

So do cartoonists. But there is a major difference between the way the majority of cartoonists deal with character and the way novelists or scriptwriters do. Novelists create individual characters. Contemporary cartoonists do not.

There are some exceptions to this general rule. Certain kinds of contemporary visual humorists do deal with individual people. Carica-ture—which lies beyond the scope of this book—relies for its humor on our recognition of the appearance of a specific individual, which the caricaturist distorts for comic effect. The same is true of most political cartooning. Comic-strip artists create memorable individual characters. A large part of the humor in strips comes from our recognition of those people. In fact, weak gag lines are often carried by the characters.

Modern magazine cartoonists sometimes deal with particular individ-uals. But when they do, they are likely to use characters that are folkloric or mythical; we'll treat them in a separate chapter. In most magazine cartoons, there simply is not enough time for the reader to understand even a little about the individual personality of the protagonists. Recog-

nition must be instant. So cartoonists use not characters, but character *types*. Readers immediately recognize the type. The cartoonist can use that recognition to induce humor.

While the use of types rather than real people may in some ways limit cartoonists, it also offers them advantages. Often the aftertaste of a good cartoon—the viewer's feeling that the cartoonist has said something universal—comes precisely because the cartoonist has used a character type. The viewer can apply the insight about the character type to individual people more easily than he or she could with a drawing of a specific person. Even viewers who in some way "fit" the type may find the cartoon funny precisely because it does not specifically lampoon them. Character types, then, are another important kind of visual cliché available to the cartoonist.

The most easily recognizable character types are people who have personality traits that everyone dislikes. High on the list of such traits is vanity. The self-inflated man or woman, the fop, the dandy—and fops and dandies come in all genders—have been targets for humor from time immemorial. The two drawings by Daumier on the following page—the woman is actually a caricature of a famous male editor—illustrate the universal appeal of this character type. The pictures are funny enough in themselves. But if we added a caption to either of them, Daumier's characters could, with little alteration, be the pretentious dowagers, ambitious social climbers, and unctuous businessmen so long lampooned in *The*

New Yorker. Redrawn, the man might even be the fop made famous as *The New Yorker*'s signature cover.

The monomaniac, fixated on one idea or occupation to the exclusion of everything else, is another common funny character type. Daumier evidently knew the fanatical fishermen of his day. Modernize the clothing, and the picture would equally well depict the single-minded fishermen of today. Change the venue to a more recently developed sport, and you might produce cartoons about fanatical golfers. Bring it right up-to-date, add a caption lampooning pretense, and you have this comment on the contemporary preoccupation with physical fitness.

"I am, of course, quite fit, or, if you prefer, extraordinarily fit, but I wouldn't say I was 'perfectly fit.'"

Monomaniacal preoccupation with sex has been a topic for visual humor since the days when satyrs chased maidens or each other across  Greek vases. Daumier again understood the character type. The English translation of the caption for this drawing reads, "A gentleman who gets hot in any season." The Rowlandson drawing here is titled "The Progress of Gallantry," but the visual double entendre in its depiction of voyeurism and lechery probably needs no caption.

Vanity and monomania may top the list of personality traits most people hate, but there are many more. Create a cartoon featuring a grump, a nincompoop, a know-it-all, a bully, a boor, a fast-talking con artist, a nitpicker, or someone with a chip on his or her shoulder, and you have an almost surefire route to a laugh.

Certain professions also lend themselves to depictions of character types. This is not to say that all people in a profession are alike. Within any given trade, of course, there are people with as many different kinds of personalities as there are in any other segment of the population. But we tend to view professionals, *in their professional roles*, as types. Cartoonists make them types by focusing on personality traits commonly associated with the profession.

The professional types most frequently depicted in cartoons are politicians. However passionate we may be about our particular candidate, we are always willing to see politicians in general pilloried. Personality traits usually associated with politicians are an open invitation to humor.

Politicians, we think, are glib flatterers. The sweet-talking official courting a peasant's vote in this drawing is as easily recognizable now as he was in Daumier's nineteenth-century France. Daumier's long-winded caption comes from a more leisurely era. Modern versions are likely to be

"My dear friend, do not think that I came here to ask you for your vote. I respect the independence of your opinions too much to do that. It is the Baroness who said to me 'Go and see poor Galouzot. Say to his wife that she is neglecting me, that I want to see her. Find out about their delightful children and say that I definitely want to have them for dinner.'"

"Fellow debtors!"

shorter, but they illustrate the identical characteristic. This cartoon is built on the same premise as the Daumier drawing: the idea that politicians try to flatter us by acting as though they are "just plain folks."

Politicians, we think, are also duplicitous. They are masters at evading issues. Or they are primarily concerned with keeping their jobs, rather than with doing anything for the public good. Or they are the servants of special interests. Or they have their hand in the public cookie jar. Or they are cardboard cutouts manipulated by people with more skill—and more smarts—who operate behind the scenes.

Other professionals are commonly believed to have more public approval than politicians, but they are also frequent targets of comic art. We suspect that the source of humor about these other professionals comes from the fact that most of us feel ambivalent about them. We can't do without them, but we're not happy doing with them either. In their

"But Senator, you must commit yourself. Yes or no?"

"Fellow-incumbents!"

"I wish they wouldn't put such big words in my speeches. I like to know what the hell I'm talking about."

"Ow—ow—OW!"
"That's great! The pain proves
it's coming out."
—Honoré-Victorin Daumier

"Boy, am I glad I'm not in
your shoes!"

professional roles, these people force us to deal with issues we wish we didn't have to face.

Dentists are a perfect example. For many people, the options of continuing to suffer a toothache and making a visit to the dentist may seem to be a Hobson's choice. Doctors are an almost equally good target for humor. Despite all the current talk about preventive medicine, the fact is that most of us only see a doctor when we're sick. And so visits to the doctor worry us. We worry about whether the doctor knows what he or she is doing. Incompetent doctors have been a subject for comic art for centuries. We worry about whether we can afford the treatment. Psychiatrists become a metaphor for worries about our own mental state—and also, perhaps, for our worries about the doctor's mental state.

"I'm putting you on two earrings."

"Amputation"—Thomas Rowlandson

Cartoons about lawyers also evoke our anxieties. Virtually all occasions on which we engage lawyers involve trouble: either anticipating it before the fact or handling it afterward. Again, we may worry that the lawyer is incompetent or will offer only obvious advice. Pretentiousness, callousness, avarice, self-seeking, ruthlessness are all characteristics frequently attributed to lawyers when they act in their professional roles. Any of these characteristics can become the basis for a cartoon about the legal profession.

Honoré-Victorin
Daumier

"Now, don't do anything till you hear from me."

The list of professionals who can become targets for comic art is as limitless as our worries. Think about bankers and you think about our financial anxieties. Think about generals and you think about our fear of war and our suspicion that generals are the only people who *like* war.

Think about police, and you think about our fears of wrongdoing, our guilt, or our anxieties about being unprotected.

In addition to professionals whom we may consult in real life, there are other professional character types we probably never actually meet that have become internal clichés in the cartooning field. The crystal-ball gazer telling us about new disasters facing us evokes our fear of the future. The flasher and the hooker become metaphors for our sexual anxieties.

As sensibilities have changed, certain character types have begun to disappear from modern cartoons. This is particularly true of stereotyped depictions of women. The bimbo, the gold digger, the dumb secretary, the vacant-minded housewife—all are, if not yet eliminated from modern cartooning, at least endangered species, the extinction of which deserves applause. Drawings of some character types have also changed over time. Politicians, for example, are likely to be drawn leaner and more telegenic than they were a generation ago. But character types still legitimately form the basis for much cartooning humor.

When novelists and screenwriters handle characters, they can and must deal in brand names. Cartoonists, on the other hand, must generally deal in generic products. But, as we all know, generic products often work just as well as brand-name items. They're also less expensive and easier to come by.

12
Visual Clichés as Idea Sources

If modern magazine cartoons are full of generic character types, all visual humor—historical and modern—is full of generic images. These images, used so often that they have become clichés, are a kind of visual shorthand. Artists use the shorthand to make abstract concepts visually concrete in an economical and powerful way.

Take the Earth, for example. A drawing of a globe makes concrete the abstraction Humanity. Thomas Nast's anti-war drawing here, which also uses visual imagery from classical antiquity, is designed to evoke a mordant, or perhaps even a despairing, laugh. It is only one example out of thousands of pictures in which the Earth is the central image.

THE ADVANCED AGE
MERCURY: "What under the sun are you doing."
MARS: "Mortals will make such big guns, and this is the consequence."
—Thomas Nast

Depictions of Peace as a dove, of Conquest, Slaughter, Famine, and Death as frightening figures on horseback, of Justice as a blindfolded woman with a scale in one hand and a law book in the other, are all familiar to cartoon viewers. Equally familiar are the visual symbols that depict the abstract notions Nation or Country: the British bulldog, the Russian bear, the American eagle.

Depiction of American eagle before and after the beginning of the Civil War —Michael Angelo Woolf

The usefulness of images like these in political cartooning is obvious. Less obvious is the fact that these generic images may form the basis for the kind of associations that generate funny drawings that are not overtly political.

For instance, let's take the two symbols most frequently used to depict the abstract concept of the United States: Uncle Sam and the Statue of Liberty. Both have appeared in innumerable political cartoons. But what happens if we take them out of their political context and turn them into ordinary human beings who do ordinary things? Because they are who they are, otherwise commonplace behaviors and utterances become funny. We might, for example, put Uncle Sam into a business context and make him into a busy executive. The result could be the top drawing opposite.

Or we might turn Uncle Sam and Ms. Liberty into a couple. How do they start their day? They have breakfast in the kitchen. Take a standard prop from the kitchen: the refrigerator with many notes hanging on the door. What kind of notes might *this* couple put on *their* fridge?

"Get me the Statue of Liberty."

If they're a couple, they're bound to suffer the kinds of conflicts other couples endure. But because they are who they are, the conflicts may take an unusual turn. Do they—like all couples—argue about money? Think about the problems the country faces, and you might emerge with the cartoon below.

"You're a fine one to talk about my spending!"

As a couple, they probably have a social life together. Perhaps she's unhappy about the way their jobs affect that social life.

"We have no friends, just allies."

*"I have something to get off my chest—I don't know the words to the
second verse of the Star-Spangled Banner."*

He may suffer from a memory lapse that is probably common to 99
percent of the American population. But because he is who he is, his
confession of the lapse makes us laugh.

If we make the pair into an old-fashioned couple where she does the
cooking and he does the eating, he might complain about the food.

"Not apple pie again!"

*"I say we renounce world leadership
and just have fun."*

Finally, on a happy-go-lucky note, she might suggest a solution to all of their problems.

Symbols such as Uncle Sam and Lady Liberty, which depict political abstractions, are not the only kinds of visual clichés that may spark ideas for magazine cartoons. Benjamin Franklin verbally conjoined two of the most important and dreaded abstractions that become concrete causes for misery in our lives when he penned his famous aphorism, "In this world, nothing is certain but death and taxes." Death and Taxes—both abstractions—have specific physical representations. The most common contemporary cartoon depiction of Death is as the Grim Reaper carrying a scythe. Taxes becomes the man in a business suit with the letters *I.R.S.* on his briefcase.

Put the two visual images together in the same picture and you have this cartoon. It is a good example of a drawing where the reader supplies the cliché. Making Uncle Sam the starter adds an additional piquancy to

the picture. Incidentally, this cartoon was printed in *The New Yorker* on the eve of the dreaded April 15 tax filing deadline, which gave it an extra fillip.

Once we have the notion that we can put these two clichéd figures in the same picture, we can generate other funny ideas. Suppose that, after each spends a day of hard work collecting souls or surcharges, the pair are drinking buddies. Put them in a bar. One says to the other, "In this age of insecurity, relativity, and moral rootlessness, it's nice to meet another certainty." Or suppose that each is not a single generic figure, but is part of a large organization of professionals who do the same kind of work. Put one of them at a podium in front of a room full of Grim Reapers and I.R.S. men. The speaker says, "My fellow certainties!"

While Death and Taxes may go together, each can be given a starring role in his own drawing. The I.R.S. man has shown up in thousands of cartoons. A personified image of Death has appeared frequently in pictures that are not designed to be humorous. But—perhaps because death

"Mr. Bismarck's Nightmare"
(Daumier depicts Death as
congratulating Bismarck
for creating so many
wars.)

evokes such anxiety in us that we want momentarily to laugh away our fear of it—Death can also provide the stimulus for many humorous illustrations. Is Death married? Perhaps his wife sends him off to work: "Have a nice day taking people to their eternal rewards and punishments, dear." Does Death have a boss who nags him about deadlines? Does he worry about getting a promotion? Does he get put "on hold"? Does he get a yearly vacation? "Relax," Death says to a man lounging on a beach, "I'm just taking a holiday, like everyone else."

That last idea illustrates another common category of cartoons about Death: pictures that show a person responding when the Grim Reaper shows up at his or her door. Character types may yield results here. A self-important tycoon, seeing the Grim Reaper, yells into the intercom: "Dammit, Miss Tyson, I told you I was not seeing *anyone*!" Or he ruefully asks his visitor, "This is it—the final takeover bid?" A busy, vain doctor tells Death, "Sorry, I don't have a free time slot for at least six months." A fearful lawyer asks, "How about a plea bargain?"

Uncle Sam, the Statue of Liberty, the Grim Reaper, and the I.R.S. man are images that are widely used in many aspects of our visual culture. But there are also some visual cliché images that—like certain settings—are more or less internal to the cartooning field. Think about a sultan riding on a flying carpet. Does he have a fully equipped bar on the carpet? A television set? A cellular phone? Put a snake charmer in front of a basket. How many responses can the snake make to the charmer's music? What else might emerge from the basket instead of a snake?

Picture an archaeologist viewing hieroglyphics on the wall of a cave or a pyramid. What (generally modern) words does he translate? Or picture a pyramid. A variation in construction might produce this cartoon. (Note that placing the rider on the camel in the foreground adds another

kind of visual cliché to the drawing and firmly anchors it in a particular geographic setting.) Staying with the funereal images, we can use tombstones to generate humorous drawings.

"Détente."

Some character types and mythical figures have also achieved the status of visual clichés. Thinking about a witch or an elf, a devil or an angel, a prisoner or a street vendor, a magician pulling a rabbit out of a hat, or rats deserting a sinking ship can evoke funny associations. As this picture—now dated but still funny—illustrates, some cartoon characters have themselves become so widely recognized that they are clichés.

Just as a cartoonist must revel in verbal clichés, so he or she must embrace visual clichés. The number of pictorial clichés that a cartoon viewer will easily recognize seems almost limitless. Newspaper editorial cartoons, books of political or nonpolitical drawings, advertisements, comic strips, and movies are all rich sources for familiar images. Or, if nothing else works, an art museum might generate funny ideas. There's just no telling what might emerge from such a place.

II
Generating Funny Ideas: Specialized Sources

In the first section of this book, we talked about general techniques of association that can be used to create funny visual ideas. We're now going to devote several chapters to specific subjects and sources for cartoon ideas. There are hundreds of such subjects and sources. We'll deal only with the most common. All of the associative techniques we've discussed—opposites and similarities, words, verbal clichés, props, characters, settings, visual clichés—can be employed to generate and develop ideas from them.

13
Fairy Tales and Nursery Rhymes

If the Freudians are right that the roots of much of our behavior lie somewhere in our earliest life experiences, then the roots of much of our sense of humor probably also lie there. Certainly some of the most promising premises for funny ideas come from our earliest years. They are fairy tales, nursery rhymes, and riddles. These premises, learned in childhood, have been lodged in our minds far below the level of consciousness. And so a twist on a tale, a rhyme, or a riddle can almost always get a laugh.

Inserting modern props into ancient tales is one way to make them funny. Inserting a modern object—the pizza box—into the familiar story of Rapunzel produced this cartoon. The technique will work equally well with other tales. Did Goldilocks use a modern burglar's kit of tools, Little Red Riding Hood a can of "Wolf-Off," Hansel and Gretel's witch a microwave oven, Little Tommy Tucker an electric guitar, the cow who jumped over the moon a space suit? Incongruous modern settings for ancient tales, like the one in the version of the Chicken Little story shown on the following page, will also generate ideas. Goldilocks, the Three Bears, or Snow White, for instance, might appear as guests on a TV talk show. Jack and the Giant might play a video game to see who gets the goose that lays golden eggs. Or try inserting professional character types. Did Cinderella hire a lawyer to prove the glass slipper belonged to her? What kind of doctor treated King Midas? After a long day working in the mines, did the Seven Dwarfs consult a chiropractor?

"The sky is falling. Details at eleven."

Reprinted courtesy *OMNI* magazine

An even more rewarding way to use these sources is to take a familiar tale or rhyme and associate about the tale in as many ways as you can. As an example, we'll take a classic fairy tale scene. The princess kisses the enchanted frog and turns him into a prince. How many twists, turns, and points of view can we take with that one premise?

First, there's the frog. Begin with his emotions. How does *he* feel about the situation? Most of us have not—at least since we were fairy-tale age—known very many frogs on a one-to-one basis, so the only way to answer the question is to anthropomorphize the frog. Since he is really a prince anyway, attributing human emotions to him seems only fair.

How does the frog feel about *princesses*? Again, we can insert one of our professional character types. Maybe the frog has princessophobia and is seeing a psychia-

Attributed to Toba Sōjō (Japanese, A.D. 1053–1140)

trist to work it out. A frog on a couch says, "I have this hostility toward

princesses." Or the shrink says, "And how long have you felt this hostility toward princesses?" The frog may fancy only certain kinds of princesses and be worried about his fetishism. He may be too shy to express his attraction to princesses. He may be very macho about them. On another track, the frog may have *political* feelings about monarchy. Perhaps he's a radical populist frog who wants nothing to do with royalty.

Attributed to Toba Sōjō (Japanese, A.D. 1053–1140)

Place the frog in a social context. All of his friends are frogs. What do *they* think about princesses? They may not approve. Have they had their own experiences with kissing princesses? They might give him advice, based on their memories of princess kissing. Are *they* politically opposed

to monarchy? Is there a Frog Liberation Front to which they belong? Or perhaps the frog's friends believe that kissing princesses is what we used to call, in the days before sexual liberation, a perversion.

Think family settings. The frog's family, like his friends, are all frogs. How does his mother feel about the situation? Did she warn her son about kissing strange princesses? She might be reluctant to have him become a prince because she has other aspirations for him. A Mom frog thinks, "My frog, the doctor." His father gives him advice: "Well, son, you're getting old enough to start thinking about princesses," or "Well, son, I think it's time you learned something about the birds, the bees, and the princesses." The frog's kid brother might rat on him: "Nyah! Nyah! Today I saw Freddy behind the castle kissing a princess." Does his older sister tease him about the princesses in his life? Perhaps he has a doting aunt, a fond uncle, a wise old grandmother or grandfather.

Put the frog in a work setting, or imagine the results of his work. Perhaps he has a job he likes and doesn't want to swap it for princing. He may worry that, in these antimonarchical times, being a prince has too little job security. He may be anxious about what his boss frog will say if he doesn't show up for work the next day. On the other hand, he may be looking for a way out of a dead-end job and think that kissing a princess is just the ticket to a new and exciting career.

The same pattern of associations will work for the princess. Does she find frogs unattractive? Or does she find *princes* unattractive? How do *her* friends feel about the situation? Perhaps one writes a graffito: Frogs are Impotent. The princess's parents—the king and queen—could have tart words to say about this particular frog, or about frogs in general. Perhaps the queen married a frog turned prince, and warns her daughter not to make the same mistake. The princess may yearn for some other job and refuse to follow in the family business of reigning.

Having filled in some of the background about the pair, try thinking about the actual event. They kiss. What if the frog does not turn into a prince, but into something else? Think about stock character types and visual clichés. Suppose the frog becomes a tax collector, a vampire, a bigger frog, a robot, an I.R.S. agent, the Grim Reaper, a different kind of animal, another princess. How do the pair react to these events? Move the setting. Put the pair on a city street rather than in the conventional rural scene. Does the frog go into a phone booth to change identities like Superman? What happens if the princess changes but the frog does not? Or if they both change?

"I do believe his voice is beginning to change."

Think backward in time from the actual event. Presumably the frog got into his pickle because of a wicked witch. How does he feel about her? Perhaps, after some adjustment, he came to *like* being a frog. What about the princess? What's happened in her life before this moment?

Think forward in time. Assume the kiss goes as expected, and the frog is now a prince. What happens next? In the traditional tale, they get married. Who marries them? Imagine the wedding guests and the reception afterward. Half of the guests—his relatives—are frogs. How do the princess's relatives react to that fact? The king, her father, says to the queen, "I don't have anything against them, but it's damn hard making small talk." Possibly the various in-laws dance together, or tell jokes to one another.

The wedding over, what happens afterward? Probably eventually he becomes king, she queen. Is it a happy relationship? He may be nostalgic for the simple, froggy days of his youth. Or he may still be a closet case

"My God! There goes middle management."

who secretly dresses in frog drag. Dad might tell the kids about the old days when he was a frog. Their son complains, "If I hear one more story about how hard he worked when he was a young frog, I'll go crazy!" The queen may blame a child's behavior on the king's froggy genes. "He certainly doesn't get that 'rivit' sound from *my* side of the family." King and queen may have in-law problems. Plug a cliché phrase into the situation. "Dammit, Gertrude," the king says, "you knew when you married me that my mother was a frog!" Follow the couple through the rest of their life cycle up to and including their deaths. What are their funerals like? Their tombstones?

One of us once sat down and, in a single idea session, created twenty-five frog and princess ideas by this kind of association. Happily for cartoonists, the frog and princess premise is only one among many that are equally familiar to contemporary audiences. Simply casting your mind back to your own childhood will probably produce enough premises to last for quite a while. The tales and rhymes you recall most easily are likely to be the ones that have the most resonance for you and therefore the ones that will most easily generate ideas. But if simple memory doesn't do the trick, consult children's books of nursery rhymes or fairy tales. Take any tale or rhyme, associate with the protagonists' emotions, with props or settings or character types, or think about the story backward and forward in time. You'll find these sources are truly enchanted. Without even so much as a kiss, they turn into wonderful cartoon ideas.

14
Myths and Legends

Closely related to nursery rhymes and fairy tales as cartoon sources are myths and legends. We learn many of these tales as children too. In fact—although earlier ages would have made less clear distinctions between "children's stories" and fiction for adults—some myths and legends are now viewed as the exclusive property of the young. Whenever we may have learned them, many are so familiar that they offer the instant recognition necessary for successful cartoons. Equally important, these tales—as do all important myths—stay in our minds because they are about themes and emotions that touch all of us.

In the United States—and probably in most Western cultures—the mythical premises used most frequently as a basis for cartoons are biblical stories. While a few New Testament images—the three wise men, for example—appear with some regularity in cartoons, it is Old Testament tales that most often provide the basis for the inversions that bring a laugh.

Some statistician of cartooning might prove us wrong, but our hunch is that the two biblical premises that are most frequently used in cartoon art are the tale of Adam and Eve in the Garden of Eden and the story of Noah's ark. Both premises have traditional depictions, and so both are examples of the visual cliché. And both stories touch on universal themes.

The cliché picture for the Adam and Eve story focuses on three stock characters and a prop. Any of them can form the basis for a cartoon idea.

The characters embody two universal themes: innocence (Adam and

Eve) and temptation (the snake). As often seems the case, temptation is more interesting than innocence. The snake rivets our attention.

In the original tale, the evil serpent lures Adam and Eve by promising them knowledge of good and evil. But suppose the serpent has more up-to-date temptations to offer: a used car driven only on Sundays by a little old lady, a never-to-be-repeated offer on an exercise machine that will take inches off your tummy when used only five minutes a day, a one-of-a-kind three-tape album of forty songs recorded by Elvis Presley after his death, a stock portfolio that will guarantee worry-free retirement for an initial investment of only $29.95 plus shipping and handling. Legitimate

cartoon ideas all. To invert the premise, we could take the modern-day tempters who might make such offers—a used-car salesman, an exercise tout, a TV announcer, a stockbroker—and put them in the tree instead of the snake.

Moving the snake is another way to invert the premise. The serpent is sufficiently familiar as a temptation image that it can be taken out of the Garden of Eden scene altogether. Put the snake in a used-car lot, twined around a bumper, and have it utter the line about the little old lady's car. Put it behind the counter in an exercise emporium and have it tempt a modern-day couch potato with the tummy-tuck machine. Expand the idea by thinking about stock characters. What temptations might the snake offer a general—"Look! Unlimited appropriations, with no congressional oversight; check it out!"—a judge—"Landmark cases each and every time!"—or a doctor—"Your very own disease named after you!"

Consider the scene's major prop. Genesis does not specify what fruit the serpent gave to Eve, and then Eve to Adam. In the King James translation of the Bible, they sample "the fruit of the tree which is in the midst of the garden." But we all "know," of course, that Eve gave Adam an apple, because visual artists have drawn the scene that way for centuries. Apples lead to other associations: apple pie (is the knowledge of good and evil as American as . . .), apple sauce, apple pandowdy. What if Adam doesn't like apples or apple sauce or apple pandowdy and Eve can't get him to bite? How would he react if she gave him a *tomato* of knowledge. A banana of knowledge? A kumquat of knowledge?

If the Adam and Eve story offers three characters and a prop, the Noah's ark tale offers characters galore. There are Noah and his wife, their children, and—most important—an almost limitless set of wildlife characters. The themes in the ark tale are different from those of the Eden story, but equally powerful: catastrophe, confinement, and, ultimately, hope.

The catastrophe theme is a particularly rich one in an era like ours where the media are full of predictions about ecological disaster. Species are endangered, we are told. Does an animal plead for a berth on the ark on the grounds that it's endangered? Maybe some species got left off the Ark altogether. Try inserting creatures now extinct into the story. How might a dodo, an auk, a saber-toothed tiger relate to Noah? Or—more fancifully—did a unicorn miss the boat? Charles Addams did a famous cartoon on that premise. A centaur or some other mythical creature might also work. What's the modern equivalent of the ark? Do people see a space shuttle with a long line of animals ready to board it? What do the people say?

Confinement is the second theme for Noah's ark humor. Everyone on the ark is cooped up together for forty long rainy days. How do they feel about that? The animals are couples. Think about domestic conflict. How would you feel if you and your partner spent forty days together cooped up on a dank little boat? What do the animal pairs say to one another? Or consider how one kind of animal might feel about being confined with its traditional enemy, say a sheep about the lions, a mouse about the cats, a cat about the dogs. Are there unpopular animals everyone else avoids, like skunks and porcupines? What if there are pairs of viruses on board?

Hope is the third theme. In the biblical tale, it comes from a dove who is sent out several times and finally returns carrying an olive branch as a sign that the flood is over. Replace the olive branch with a different prop—a television set, a tax form, a guided missile, an offer for Noah to publish a book. What does the dove say? What does Noah say?

The ark and the garden are only the most frequently used biblical stories. The various tales about Moses have furnished many cartoon ideas. The story about him parting the Red Sea invites the insertion of modern props, as in this cartoon. The image of Moses carrying stone tablets containing the ten commandments conjures up many themes: authority and our reactions to it, fudging on rules, negotiation, trying to make deals. It may also suggest modern technology. Perhaps Moses carries not stone tablets, but a computer floppy disk. Or he gets the message from a fax machine. Jonah and the whale, Samson and Delilah, and David and Goliath are other examples of biblical images that are frequently the subject of cartoons.

Myths from classical antiquity also form a part of the humorous artist's store of easily recognizable images. When using these myths, though, a modern cartoonist is at something of a disadvantage compared with earlier visual humorists. In the United States at least, the number of such myths that are widely recognized has become fewer and fewer. When Daumier drew this picture, for example, he could assume that his viewers were familiar with the story of Cornelia,

Honoré-Victorin
Daumier

the "mother of the Gracci" who was much admired by the Romans as the epitome of maternal virtue. Cornelia called her children "her jewels." A modern cartoonist cannot assume such familiarity. Even the story of Achilles, who was dipped by his mother in waters that made him invulnerable except for the spot on his heel where she held him, is, we think, on the margins of recognition for modern audiences.

But some classical myths are still alive and well. The Trojan horse, a staple of comic drawings in an earlier period as this Thomas Nast picture illustrates, is still widely recognized as a symbol of treachery. The premise practically begs for variations. One might substitute other animals, or even objects, for the horse. How would the Trojans have reacted to a wooden walrus, gerbil, aardvark, or pussy cat? To a giant Trojan computer or fax machine? Put yourself into the shoes—or sandals—of the warriors inside the horse. Are they pleased when they're offered coffee, tea, and soft drinks? Irritated because they've already seen the movie being shown? Worried about whether they'll be on time to make their connection to the next horse? Put the concept of a treacherous gift into a modern context and see what happens. Perhaps a bevy of avaricious leveraged buyout entrepreneurs emerge from a Trojan horse in some corporate boardroom.

Daumier's depiction of Sisyphus, the ancient Greek character who is doomed forever to push the same rock up the same hill, is as relevant to politics today as it was in his time. Creatures like unicorns and centaurs

"Any Thing to Get In"

still populate modern humorous drawing, and occasionally even a satyr or two show up in a picture. The Gordian knot, supposedly cut, rather than untied, by Alexander the Great, is recognizable, as are Zeus on Mount Olympus clutching his thunderbolts and Poseidon rising from the ocean clutching his trident.

Similarly, archetypical and legendary figures and tales from the Middle Ages appear frequently in contemporary cartoons. Knights and dragons are still in good repute. The story of King Arthur and the Round Table, familiar not only through children's books but from musicals like *Camelot*, allows the modern cartoonist to make funny comments about camaraderie, bravery, and group loyalty. The specific image of the sword in the stone, which only King Arthur could remove, can be reprised in many variants. Perhaps today the sword would be a computer program, a multimillion-dollar contract for an athlete, or, in a politically-oriented picture, the national deficit (who could pull *that* one out?). Robin Hood and his men go merrily on through modern cartooning, though nowadays they most likely will have to check in with the Internal Revenue Service every April 15.

   In general, when using myths and legends—whether biblical, classical, or more recent—it's a good idea to stay with the stories you remember well. Chances are if you can't recall much of the tale, your viewers won't either. Still, a book like *Brewer's Dictionary of Phrase & Fable*, which lists hundreds of stories and references, is helpful to get the creative juices flowing. It may also remind you of the details of a tale that are just on the edge of your memory. It may also start you thinking about odd and fruitful juxtapositions. What would happen if Sisyphus pushed his rock onto Noah's ark, and the whole thing, animals and all, sank?

15
Literature, Movies, and Art

There's an ancient joke about Shakespeare's plays. A couple emerges from a theater where they have just seen *Hamlet*. "Wasn't that wonderful?" she says. "I don't know," he says with a shrug. "All the author did was sling together a whole lot of clichés."

The joke has a kernel of pure gold for a cartoonist. Great works of literature—as well as famous movies and fine pieces of art—are a rich lode of material for the visual artist precisely because so many parts of them have achieved the familiarity of clichés. As is the case with classical myths, a modern cartoonist may have a more limited set of symbols and tales that readers will easily recognize than did earlier artists. But there is still an enormous store of artistic lore that is widely known in the culture. Cartoon viewers are obviously familiar with much more than they have ever actually read or seen. To create humor from these sources, one needs only to employ the same basic association devices we have been using all along: words, clichés, settings, props, character types.

Let's stay with the Bard and *Hamlet* for a moment. Begin with the words. Perhaps no work of art has more lines that have made their way into common language. "To be or not to be: that is the question," Hamlet broods. Make Hamlet a compulsive organizer, and insert a prop in his office. "Neither a borrower nor a lender be," Polonius advises his son. Does Polonius qualify his advice? "Neither a borrower nor a lender be. Depending, of course, on the current prime rate." Take Polonius's line out of the play. Borrowing and lending suggest banks. Does a modern bank

"The Laughing Audience"
—William Hogarth

employee have a sign with Polonius's words tacked above his desk, and does his or her banker boss have a sarcastic remark to make about it? "Something is rotten in the state of Denmark," says a minor character. Hamlet presumably agrees. What if Hamlet were a modern-day politician? He and his opponent are in a televised debate. His opponent says: "I'm willing to admit that Denmark has problems, perhaps serious problems, maybe even major problems. But my opponent is engaging in negative campaigning when he says that things in Denmark are 'rotten.' "

Move from the words to the title character. Hamlet is a model of indecision. He spends five acts brooding about what he should do. Do the other characters have something to say about that? Hamlet is also a perfect example of a boy who has a troubled relationship with his Mom. What kind of Mother's Day card did Hamlet send Gertrude? Was it the same one Oedipus sent *his* mother? Perhaps Hamlet is on the couch to deal with his Mom problem. The shrink thinks, "If I hear one more word about his

"A Midsummer's-Night Dream Nomination"
Thomas Nast caricature, with The Greenback Party
as Bottom

goddamn mother, *I'll* go mad." In a more modern idiom, the psychiatrist might have something to say about Hamlet's difficulty in adjusting to his new blended family. Think about the cliché visual images in the play. The ghost appears on the ramparts. Hamlet holds up the skull of poor Yorick.

At the end of the play, everyone lies dead on the stage. What variations on the traditional story do they suggest?

Other Shakespeare plays offer similar options for twists on characters, words, props. Did King Lear's financial adviser convince him to take advantage of a wonderful early retirement plan? What kind of Father's Day cards did *Lear's* daughters send *him*? Did Lady Macbeth find a strong but oh-so-mild detergent to wash out the "damned spot"? Cassius in *Julius Caesar* has a "lean and hungry look." Obviously he needs advice from a qualified and fully certified nutritionist. For that matter—although for opposite reasons—so does Falstaff. A worried Romeo might write to Dear Abby and complain about how his girlfriend's family just doesn't seem to like him. Or a plaintive Juliet might sing "Why must I be a teenager in love?"

While Shakespeare, of course, is the bedrock of English-speaking literature, other works of serious fiction abound with ideas for visual humor. In these days of sound bites, not too many people plow through Melville's *Moby-Dick*, but Captain Ahab's quest for the white whale is still a familiar cartoon premise. We know about the captain's emotions. How does the whale feel about the matter? Put him on a psychiatrist's couch and have the shrink utter a reassurance: "Not to worry. Many white whales have a harmless delusion that they're being pursued by a mad sea captain." For another animal character, you might try Poe's raven, who

obviously needs an improve-your-vocabulary course. Joseph Keppler, a nineteenth-century American artist, used the raven metaphor to picture a disagreement over American tariff policy.

No cartoonist has ever said "Bah! Humbug!" to Scrooge or to Bob Cratchit and Tiny Tim; they are too useful as subjects for funny art. Washington Irving's Rip Van Winkle—who these days might be doing advertisements for sleeping pills—suggests jokes about sleep, insomnia, and waking up in the wrong place (or time). Jonathan Swift's Lilliputians from *Gulliver's Travels* have made more than tiny inroads into the business of humorous illustration. Don Quixote could tilt at tax collectors, advertisers, crooked politicians, or the national budget as well as at windmills.

For the same reason that nursery rhymes provide good sources for cartoons, children's literature is a fertile field for funny sprouts. Did Peter Rabbit and Mr. MacGregor eventually reach a negotiated settlement? Perhaps Flopsy, Mopsy, and Cottontail went on to become a famous female vocal trio. As they all sit in a retirement home, do they fondly reminisce about their youthful adventures? Peter Pan never did grow up, but what about Captain Hook? Eventually the Captain probably retired too. Perhaps he wrote a book about the "Pan Problem" and appeared on TV talk shows to promote it. Alice's Wonderland adventures can appear in many guises in cartoons. The White Rabbit trades in his pocket watch for a digital timepiece. A business tycoon shouts, "Off with their heads." Maybe Alice, like Captain Hook, wrote a book. The Scarecrow, the Tin Man, and the Cowardly Lion were looking for brains, a heart, and courage. But what if they were searching for a cure for inflation and the Wizard of Oz claimed he had found one? That would make the Wizard an even bigger con man than he already is. Follow Peter Rabbit down into Wonderland, have him join Tinkerbell, let them all follow the Yellow Brick Road, and see what emerges.

Some literary characters are so well known that they have become generic character types. Bram Stoker's *Dracula* is the prototype for all subsequent vampires. What would a contemporary nutritionist do with *his*

dietary problem? Mary Shelley's Dr. Frankenstein and the monster he created—really a quite gentle creature in the tale—lurk somewhere in the background of virtually all subsequent monster figures. With a switch in characters, the brainy detective—epitomized perhaps, by Agatha Christie's Hercule Poirot—became the basis for this cartoon. Hard-boiled detectives of the kind created by Dashiell Hammett and Raymond Chandler are equally good premises. We might try the principle of opposites with them. What's the character type that is most different from a hard-boiled detective? Arguably, it's a stuffed animal. A teddy bear, fedora hat on his head and a cigarette dangling from his lips, sits at a desk that has a whisky bottle on it. He eyes a Barbie doll sitting in the chair across from him and thinks, "From the moment this babe walked into my office, I knew she spelled trouble."

Vampires, monsters, and detectives, of course, have also been adapted as standard fare in movies. But original films—particularly "classic" ones—can also provide a rich supply of characters, lines, and settings for

"The fact that you, Frothingham, claimed you discovered the body at exactly 12:13 P.M. was what first made me suspicious, of course. And then when Billington claimed that he had heard the clock chime the quarter hour just as he and Miss Arbuthnot met for their little assignation in the study, it was clear that you, Merryweather . . ."

cartoons. King Kong has hung from the Empire State building in many drawings. "Frankly, Scarlett, I don't give a damn," Rhett says in *Gone with the Wind*. What if he did? Or she didn't? "Play it again, Sam," Rick says in *Casablanca*. (Actually that's not exactly what he said, but that's the way the line has come down as a cliché.) What if Sam played Beethoven's Ninth Symphony or an Elvis Presley hit?

"Play it, Sam."

Familiar works of visual art also invite cartoon treatment. Our guess is that a contest to pick the visual artwork most frequently used in cartoons would end in a toss-up between Leonardo da Vinci's painting of the Mona Lisa and Rodin's sculpture of the Thinker.

Poor Mona has smiled her way through innumerable funny variations. What amused her? Perhaps Leonardo accidentally did something she found slightly humorous. Did he slip on a banana peel? Wear socks that didn't match? Leave his fly unzipped? Or perhaps he *tried* to get her to smile. "Did you hear the one about the elephant and the giraffe?" he says. Maybe her smile was only the result of indigestion. Alter Mona's expression, and you might give her more emotional range. Does she laugh uproariously? Frown? Grimace? Thumb her nose? If so, why?

The Thinker, who suggests our own thought processes, invites us to use the contrasting opposites of important and trivial. He looks so serious. But he may really be thinking—as most of us do much of the time—about something quite mundane. A thought balloon shows him worrying: "Did I remember to turn my underwear right-side out when I put it in the laundry hamper?" "Will they discover that I've been using the office phone for personal calls?" "What if Mom finds out I'm sitting here without any clothes on?" Since the posture of the Thinker is so unmistakable, it can be transferred to other characters. Draw a monkey in the same posture who thinks about a bunch of bananas, an astronaut who worries about whether he paid his telephone bill before he left home, a business executive who broods about a corporate takeover.

Whistler's painting of his mother also gets a fair amount of cartoon attention, probably because the portrait is an open invitation to use the same premise as Hamlet jokes: a boy's relationship with Mom. The Mother sits for her portrait and thinks "He paints my portrait, but he never comes over for dinner on Sundays." Or Whistler thinks, "It's not enough I come for dinner every damn Sunday. Now she wants me to paint her damn portrait." George Washington has crossed the Delaware speaking many different lines. Monet's water lilies and haystacks have thought deep thoughts.

Cartoons that deal with viewing or reading works of art have also been a staple of visual comedy for years. Art critics—professional or amateur—have been a recurrent subject. Revenge is as sweet for visual humorists as for anyone else. Audiences are funny too. Picture a movie theater and insert odd characters. Gorillas leaving a theater sadly wipe tears from their eyes. They have just seen *King Kong*. Inside a movie theater, a group of monsters, ghouls, and vampires cheer and laugh. They

Honoré-Victorin
Daumier

Thomas
Rowlandson

are, of course, watching a horror movie. In an art museum, the father of a family of frogs points proudly to an Impressionist painting of water lilies and says, "Your great-great-grandfather lived right there."

And, of course, writers, painters, and performers are themselves legitimate subjects for humor. A muse gives an author bad advice. A painter looks at a beautiful scene and paints "ashcan" art. A clown complains to a marriage counselor that his wife does not take him

"The Chamber of Genius"
—Thomas Rowlandson

 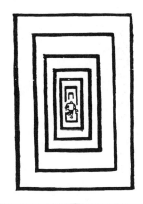 

seriously. The traditional actor's good-luck wish, "Break a leg," comes from the mouth of one of a pair of circus elephants, performing dolphins, or executioners. A street-corner artist makes a pretentious statement about her art.

From a very young age, we're instructed to take a serious, even somber, approach to great works of art. Maybe in general that's not a bad notion. But for cartoonists who are creating ideas, it's a mistake. Funny ideas abound in great art. And we can't believe that Shakespeare—who got off some of the great laugh lines of all time—would be upset if we found a chuckle or two even in *Hamlet*.

16
Historical
Characters and Settings

"Those who cannot remember the past," the philosopher George Santayana observed, "are condemned to repeat it." Cartoonists, whether or not they ever learn to avoid the errors of the past, repeatedly use settings and characters from other times. Historical images are themselves ancient as a vehicle for humorous artists.

The historical past that cartoonists portray, however, is not the same past as the one to which historians devote themselves. One of us is professionally trained as a historian. But when he sits down to create historical cartoon ideas, he deliberately sheds all of his training. For historical characters or settings in cartoons have only a remote resemblance to actual historical people or places. What cartoonists deal with when they use historical material are not the complex multiple realities of history itself, but *images* of history. The images are what remain in our minds from reading history books or historical novels, watching historical movies, seeing historical "reconstructions" on TV. They are really akin to the myths and legends we discussed in an earlier chapter.

Not only are historical cartoons seldom about the realities of history. They are seldom about history at all. Historical cartoons are almost always about the here and now. The technical device most often used in historical cartoons is anachronism: inserting something—an object, a phrase, an attitude—from one time period (usually modern) into a different era where it doesn't belong. Simple anachronism, though, doesn't necessarily

149

"The Tammany Tiger Loose"
—Thomas Nast

produce humor. Draw a sleek, contemporary automobile and put it in an early twentieth-century setting along with many Model-T cars. The modern vehicle looks odd and incongruous, but the picture is not funny. To be funny, the anachronism must make a comment about our contemporary lives.

As an example of the successful use of anachronism for humor consider the most frequently used historical cartoon premise: the caveperson. Recent research has revealed much about the way our historical ancestors probably actually lived. That research bears no relationship at all to the cavepeople cartoonists draw. Cartoon cavepersons may be dressed in loincloths, have long hair, and live in primitive conditions (all possibly historical realities). But they behave in modern ways, use modern locutions, have modern worries, express modern attitudes.

A caveman chips away at a block of stone. When he finishes, he has carved it into a crude circular shape. The premise is one of the most common for caveperson cartoons. It depicts a momentous, if mythical, event in human history: the invention of the wheel. What happens after our caveman has produced his wheel? He thinks a moment, gets an image of a modern-day traffic jam, and throws the wheel in the garbage. Or, without thinking about anything, he throws the wheel in the garbage and carves something else: a guided missile, a microwave oven, a junk-food package. Or he says a line to a cave friend about the wheel: "Research and

Development likes it, but the boys in Marketing aren't sure it has commercial appeal."

Our cavewoman draws pictures on the wall of a cave. In the middle of her crude representations of mammoths, bison, and saber-toothed tigers, she inserts an anachronism: the Mona Lisa, a Picasso-like abstract drawing, the logo or trademark for a contemporary product, Einstein's famous equation, $E = mc^2$. What then? Her friend says something disparaging about the odd addition. A committee of art critics (perhaps from the Neanderthal Endowment for the Arts) give it the "thumbs-down" gesture. Perhaps she censors herself, erases the anachronism, and replaces it with a more conventional cave drawing.

The humor in these cartoon ideas is all built by attributing to our cavepeople very modern concerns—which they could not possibly actually have had—about the less savory parts of modern everyday life, like traffic jams, the less savory parts of modern creative life, like art critics, the less savory parts of modern public life, like wars and guided missiles.

Two dinosaurs look at cavemen and -women lighting a fire. (Dinosaurs, of course, were extinct long before the first humans appeared, but that untidy historical fact is not relevant in cartooning.) One dinosaur says to the other (about the fire), "It's pretty and all that, but as far as I can see it has no practical use at all." The same pair of dinosaurs observes a group

"Dear, you forgot to put the cat out."

*"I predict that Scythia, Arabia, Babylonia, Phrygia will
always be trouble spots."*

of cavepeople throwing rocks at one another in a fierce battle. One says,
"My guess is that before too long they'll be extinct."

These cartoon ideas illustrate another device frequently used with
historical humor. They are funny in part because we know something the
characters in the drawings don't know. Giving the audience information—
or assuming that the audience has information—that the characters lack is
a device that is frequently employed in many art forms. In fiction, plays,
and films, the technique is most often used to create suspense. The
audience knows that the fearful monster or the murderer is waiting in the
heroine's path, but the heroine doesn't. The special knowledge draws

viewers into the scene. In the dinosaur cartoons, what the audience knows is not what is going to happen immediately to a heroine, but what has actually happened over thousands, even millions, of years. We know that fire is useful. And we know that—for the moment, at least—it is dinosaurs, not humans, who have become extinct.

Some critics call this technique "superiority humor." They assert that we often laugh to make ourselves feel superior to other people. Such superiority humor has been used in many kinds of cartoons. A famous set of insurance ads, for example, showed characters with disasters about to happen to them—a piano about to fall, a wrecking ball about to destroy an office—with the caption, "My insurance company? Why it's . . ." But the superiority we feel because of a sense of long history is richer in overtones than most other feelings of superiority, and so this comic technique has a special piquancy in historical gags.

The best historical cartoons have an aftertaste that probably comes from the viewer's ironic recognition of the truth of the French proverb, "Plus ça change, plus c'est la même chose." ("The more things change, the more they remain the same.") Take this cartoon, which relies on superiority humor for its effect. From our superior later perspective, we know that the areas in the Middle East about which the Roman senator is pontificating will, in fact, continue to be "trouble spots" for two millennia or more. Things stay the same. Or they fall apart the same way.

A similar aftertaste can be achieved with other anachronisms. Earlier we discussed politicians who try to ingratiate themselves into our favor by claiming that they are just ordinary folk. The historical cartoon here implies that such politicians have always been with us. Try inserting other

"*Fellow barbarians!*"

such universal character types into historical settings. Was there an oily salesman who sold used chariots in the Roman Empire, an overenthusiastic travel agent who touted the glories of the Crusades during the Middle Ages, a zealous entrepreneur who tried to sell stock in the company that built the Great Wall in ancient China? Cartoonists can also use generic historical figures to suggest such universality, as Thomas Nast did in the cartoon below lampooning the—apparently universal— phenomenon of politicians on the take.

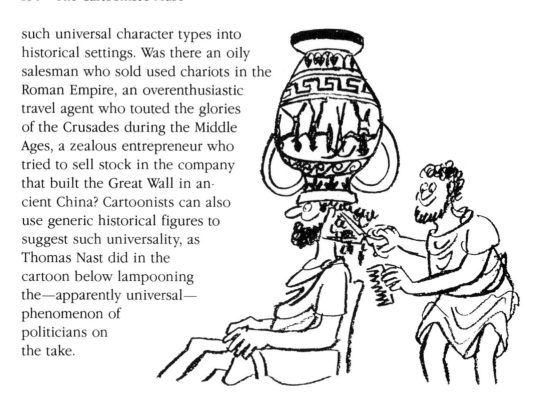

Some specific historical figures are also stock images for cartoons. In some cases, like Richard III, they have become metaphors for repulsive personal characteristics, as in this cartoon, which depicts Andrew Jackson as that rapacious monarch. Most treatments of historical figures are more benign. Poor Isaac Newton has had hundreds of apples dropped on his head in hundreds of cartoons. Benjamin Franklin has flown his kite, George Washington has confessed to cutting down the cherry tree, Napoléon has stood with his hand inside his coat, and Abraham Lincoln has chopped wood in many more. Take a recognizable historical figure, give him or her some modern props or concerns, and you have a

"You never remember my birthday!"

new historical gag. Did Attila the Hun hire a media consultant to polish his image? Did Nero, watching a city burn, wonder if his fiddling would make the Roman Top Forty? As a Roman gladiator entered the Coliseum to fight, perhaps he said to another gladiator, "Well, break a leg!"

Or take historical figures who, if they existed at all, lived so far in the past that we can only imagine them. The first amphibious creature to climb up out of the sea and start the long process of evolution on land would be a renowned historical figure if anyone knew who it was. Did the creature's mom insist that it put on its galoshes? Give it a lunch bucket? Remind it to call home every Sunday? The first ape to get up off all fours and stand erect would be equally famous if we knew who it was. But there must have been diehards who thought that bipedalism was merely a passing fad.

The glory of historical cartoons is that they can range over the whole expanse of human—and pre-human—history. The paradoxical reality of such cartoons is that they are, forever and always, set in the present.

"Well, I think we might not go too far in drawing at least two conclusions about them. They were gigantic in size and addicted to gambling."

Thomas Nast

Thomas Nast

17
Animals

In what ways are animals different from human beings? For centuries, sages and savants have speculated about that issue. In its place, it's a proper and intriguing question. But for cartoonists, it's the wrong question. A cartoonist should begin with the proposition that animals are *like* human beings, and then try to find ways to illustrate that truism. For when we laugh at animal cartoons, we are seldom laughing at animals. We are almost always laughing at people. In cartoons—as in other forms of art—animals are metaphors for human fears, human hopes, human foibles.

Many famous comic-strip characters are, of course, animals who have human characteristics. And we are all familiar with the use of animals in drawings as symbols for human institutions. The Republican party's elephant and the Democratic party's donkey are but two of the most familiar animal images of this kind. The depiction of an individual as an animal, whether for flattery or for scorn, is an equally familiar device of visual humor.

In most magazine cartooning, though, animals are not used so directly. We've found that when we associate about animal ideas for humorous illustrations, it's most productive to think in a more

"Zig-Zag Simian"—J. A. Shepherd (British, nineteenth century)

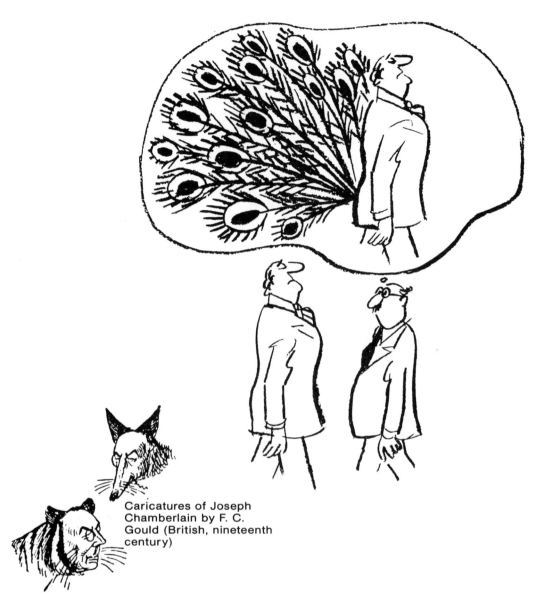

Caricatures of Joseph
Chamberlain by F. C.
Gould (British, nineteenth
century)

generic way. That is, we try to find animal traits that are recognizably like
human traits, and then translate them into cartoon form.

To begin our discussion of this kind of animal drawing, we'll take the
creatures most commonly used in general cartoons: dogs and cats. And to
avoid offending people on either side of the Great Domestic Animal
Question, we'll devote equal time to each kind of pet. Both, incidentally,
elicit high passion in cartoon viewers. There's an old saw in the comic-
strip business that says you should always put a dog or a cat in your strip,
because if a newspaper drops the feature, dog fanciers or cat lovers will
set up a tremendous howl (or caterwaul, as the case may be) and the
newspaper will have to reinstall the strip.

What's humanlike about dogs and cats? Many things, of course. Part of the appeal of dogs is that they are generally supposed to be friendly. But friendship, as we all know, is not always the perfect blendship. Cartoon dogs may worry about the nature of their friendships and seek professional help. A cartoon dog might rebel against the traditional acts of

"O.K., who else has experienced the best-friend relationship as inadequate?"

"Why, it's empty!"

friendship it is supposed to perform. The proverbial St. Bernard rescue dog might take a different view of its lifesaving mission with brandy. Or, on a domestic note, a dog may not like bringing the master a newspaper or slippers. It may read the newspaper or don the slippers itself. Perhaps several dogs want to negotiate for a fairer deal in performing friendship tasks. Picture a negotiating table with dogs on one side, masters on the other, and piles of slippers and newspaper in the middle. Do the dogs hire a lawyer to represent them in their negotiations? Do they picket when they don't get their way? In a more sympa-thetic mode, a dog might worry about the effect of its kind acts on its best friend. A pooch tells the master, "I threw out the newspaper. When you read it, you just get depressed."

"If I take too many naps during the day, I find it difficult to sleep at night."

Cats appeal to us partly because they are unabashedly sybaritic; we have yet to meet a Puritan cat. For example, who has not envied a cat its ability to relax? But suppose a cat has a very human problem with sleep-ing. Cats are notorious for being preoccupied with food. They can become metaphors for every human problem with eating. By a rough estimate, at least 50 percent of the jokes in one of the most famous cat comic strips are about gluttony. The opposite of gluttony, as most people who share a house with a cat—no one *owns* a cat—have discovered, is pickiness about food. Perhaps a cat, looking at a food dish, confides to another, "Just to keep them off balance, every once in a while, I gobble up the whole

disgusting mess." Think about other behavioral characteristics of the two animals—tail wagging or purring, burying bones or scratching sofas; going for a walk with someone or refusing to pay any attention to some-one—and find the human analogues.

From the behavioral characteristics of cats and dogs, it is easy to pad on over cliché phrases and pictures about the animals. We go to the dogs, drink the hair of the dog that bit us, get put in the doghouse, let sleeping dogs lie, die like dogs. We take catnaps, make cats' cradles, see how the cat jumps, let the cat out of the bag, play while the cat's away, pay big money for a jewel that is described as a cat's eye. People wear dog tags. Do dogs ever wear people tags? People utter catcalls when they don't like a performer. How do cats express similar displeasure? "It's a dog's life," we say. Does a dog think a people's life is equally as bad? Do cats make peopley remarks about other cats? Does a middle-aged dog yearn for the wonderful days of puppy love? Perhaps a canine senior citizen wife reflects another cliché when she speaks to her mate: "So what if you can't learn any new tricks. You've still got a damn fine retirement plan." A feline senior citizen reflects about her lives: "Once I got through those damn midlife crises in numbers five, six, and seven, numbers eight and nine have been simply splendid."

Mix and match the clichés. "It's raining cats and dogs," we complain. What if it literally rained cats and dogs? How would the cats and dogs feel about that? Or suppose it rained people. Is a cat offended by being offered food from a doggy bag? A dog by someone accusing him of playing "a cat and mouse game"?

From clichés, we can move on little cat's feet to dogs and cats made famous in literature, movies, history, nursery rhymes, fairy tales, myths. Does Lassie have a beeper that tells her when she's supposed to come home? The Cheshire Cat appears and disappears. Perhaps that creates an

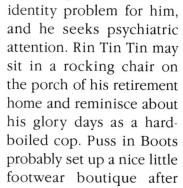

identity problem for him, and he seeks psychiatric attention. Rin Tin Tin may sit in a rocking chair on the porch of his retirement home and reminisce about his glory days as a hard-boiled cop. Puss in Boots probably set up a nice little footwear boutique after retirement. The cat may take his fiddle and hey-diddle-diddle trying to get a job with a symphony orchestra, while the little dog laughs to see such fun.

If putting on the dog with feline and canine premises is the cat's meow, there are many other domesticated animals that are almost equally rich in associations for creating funny drawings. A few quite ordinary domesticated animals are, somehow, intrinsically funny. As we noted earlier, goldfish in bowls are intrinsically funny. Although we may have to ruminate for a time to discover why, cows also seem intrinsically funny. So do goats. Put the two animals together, and you get this cartoon. Horses may be less funny now than they were a century or so ago when they were the universal means of transportation, but we have seen many successful horse ideas.

Wild animals are also good sources for humor. Our impression is that—perhaps because we know them less well than their domestic cousins—they tend to have fewer recognizable characteristics that can become premises for gags. Often, though, the traits they do have offer a great many possibilities for variations.

Some animals—and we're using "animals" here to include all living creatures—have pronounced physical characteristics with human analogues that make good cartoons. From a human point of view, for example, giraffes are virtually all neck. They lend themselves to cartoons about

*"I may be biased,
but I believe goat cheese is superior."*

neckwear. Did Uncle Elmo send our giraffe an ugly necktie that the poor
creature has to wear every time Uncle comes to Sunday dinner? Or did
Aunt Matilda knit a scarf? Octopuses have tentacles. The human analogues
are fingers. Perhaps octopus pianists can only play eight-to-the-bar.

*"I would like to thank my owners, my trainer, my
jockey, and everyone in my stable, without whom
my victory would not have been possible."*

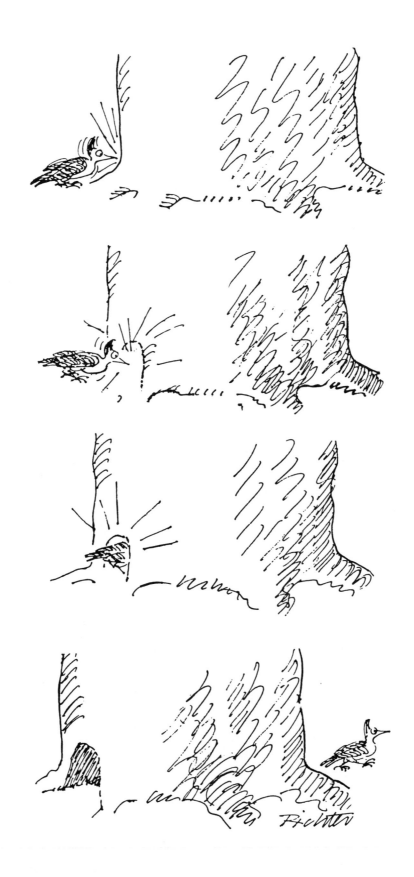

Kangaroos' pouches have a human analogue in pockets or purses. Does Ms. Kangaroo find it impossible to find her keys in her pouch, have it overflowing with tissue because she has a cold, secrete a can of mace in her pouch as protection against possible muggers? The pouch is also Baby Kangaroo's room. The visual possibilities with that conceit are enormous. Maybe there's a television set in the "room," with an antenna that protrudes from the pouch, or a tape recorder "box" playing music that Mom finds unattractive. School-age kangaroos may want to bring friends home to their room. Mom may insist that the room be cleaned first. Or maybe baby isn't so baby anymore and takes a kangaroo of the opposite sex home to the "room."

Wild animals have distinctive attributes of *behavior* that have human parallels too. People sleep. Bears hibernate. A bear might watch the late, late fall show before dozing off for a good winter's hibernation. It might set the alarm for early April, or leave a wake-up call. It might worry about nightmares. An ursine Hamlet broods, "To hibernate: perchance to dream: ay, there's the rub." Wolves howl at the moon. People sing. Might a wolf pack read their howls from a musical score? Might they have a conductor? Might a wolf have to audition in order to howl with a particular pack? Or might some pack members want to make some other kind of music? Several wolves, all howling, glare at one who plays an accordion. The notion of "Lady of Spain" drifting across the frozen Arctic tundra is enough to make anyone howl.

The store of clichés about wild animals is perhaps not quite as rich as that about domesticated creatures, but it offers many cartoon ideas. Busy as a bee. Are all bees "Type A" personalities? What about a lazy bee? Eager as a beaver. Think opposites. A female beaver may complain to a friend

"Care to join us? We're going to sweep majestically across the plains."

"Oh, shucks! Dog bite it! Gosh! Mercy me!"

about her husband, "Let me tell you, he's not so eager when he hops into the sack." Stubborn as a mule. "Dammit, Mildred," a mule husband says. "I am simply expressing my firmly held beliefs. I am not being stubborn." Try sly as a fox, quiet as a mouse, slow as a snail, horny as an old goat, slippery as an eel, happy as a lark, crazy as a loon, and see what emerges about *people* who are sly, quiet, slow, horny, slippery, happy, or crazy.

And, of course, wild animals appear in myths, legends, nursery rhymes, riddles, and fiction. The Three Bears may be pictured on the cover of a national tabloid. "Family Home Invaded by Mysterious Blond Creature Believed to Be of Extraterrestrial Origin," reads the headline. Or they may sign a multimillion-dollar movie contract for their story. A chicken may refuse to tell why it crossed the road "for reasons of national security," or it may tell another chicken it's going to stonewall when the press asks a question about the issue. A mouse on a psychiatrist's couch may feel guilty because on Christmas Eve it feels an irresistible urge to stir. A lion may update his title: "From now on, please call me the CEO of the jungle." Perhaps a groundhog gets a job at a TV station as a weather forecaster, a hard-boiled animal detective is assigned to solve the Case of

"Of course, we could adopt some."

Cock Robin, the March Hare sets up shop as a psychiatrist, Reynaud the Fox goes into the used-car business, Smokey the Bear becomes a fire insurance agent.

Our fellow living creatures allow us to see ourselves in new and funny lights. Because of the wide variety of their recognizable physical characteristics and because there are so many clichés and stories about them, they are possibly the most fecund single category of premises for

the generation of cartoon concepts. If you run low on ideas for animal drawings, check out the "Animals, Insects" entry in *Roget's Thesaurus*, which has several pages listing birds, mammals, insects, and reptiles, or look under animal names in a dictionary of clichés or fables. Pick a creature that seems intriguing.

Then let cartooning bring out the animal in you.

18
Legitimate Switches

If imitation is the sincerest form of flattery, it is also the basis for no small amount of art. One of the most common starting points for someone who is learning to draw, to write, or to compose is to imitate past masters in the field. That's not a bad way to begin to learn cartooning either. But in cartooning, there is also a special kind of imitation that is not limited to beginners. It is the use of other people's cartoons as a starting point for original ideas of one's own. The technique is called the "legitimate switch." One takes an extant cartoon and changes—switches—one or more elements. If the changes produce a genuinely new idea, the cartoonist has gone beyond imitation to generation. The switch is "legitimate."

Legitimate switches are a standard idea-generating technique for many humorous artists.

The switch can begin with virtually any cartoon or cartoon premise. As an example, we'll start with one of the hoariest of cartoon situations. Imagine a picture. A group of people of various ages sit in a lawyer's office. The lawyer says, "Your uncle left a very unusual will." By themselves, the picture and the caption are not funny. But the situation contains an element of conflict. The heirs presumably want to inherit the dead uncle's property and don't want anyone else to do so. As we've said, conflict is always a good launching point for a cartoon. The picture also provides a setting, a collection of characters including a principal (the lawyer) and a caption. Any of these elements can become the basis for switches.

171

"Botheration"—
Thomas Rowlandson

Leave the caption, the characters, and the setting as they are, and switch the picture by adding one new element: a prop. The basic situation is conflict. What props suggest conflict? Put several pairs of boxing gloves on the lawyer's desk. The picture with its caption becomes funny. Switch the prop. Instead of the boxing gloves, add dueling pistols. Replace them with swords or water guns or bows and arrows or darts. Try a roulette wheel, a deck of cards, a video game, a Monopoly set. Simply by switching props, we've created ten new cartoon ideas. Not all of them are equally funny, but all are legitimate new concepts.

Add a different kind of prop. Have the lawyer hold the will in his hand so the viewer can see it. What does it look like? The will has a picture of a man sticking out his tongue and wiggling his fingers in his ears. Or, on a cruder note, it shows a man viewed from the rear, with his pants dropped, mooning the heirs. In a different cartoon, the will might have written messages: "I figured out how to take it with me." "I spent every damn cent of it." "You're in for a big surprise, you greedy bastards!" More new ideas, all still using the original caption.

Forget props, leave the setting and the caption intact, but insert a new character. Suppose what was unusual about the uncle's will was the object of his beneficence, and that the object is present among the human heirs. Insert an animal: a dog, a cat, a horse, a gerbil, a goldfish in a bowl, a giraffe, a cow. Or insert unusual human characters, like a mafioso or a belly dancer or a hooker. Additional cartoons.

New props or characters may also suggest a switch on the caption. Suppose we put a pile of rocks and a sledgehammer in the picture as props. "As you know," the lawyer says, "your late uncle refused to give a cent to anyone who wouldn't do an honest day's work." Add a space creature to the picture and change the caption. "As you know, your late uncle was a strong believer in Unidentified Flying Objects." Or, to go a bit further afield, add a sheep to the picture. "As you know," the lawyer says, "your late uncle had somewhat unusual sexual preferences."

Leave the characters and the caption alone, but switch the setting. Try a track and field stadium. Put a pile of money at one end of the track and the heirs at the other. The lawyer holds a starting gun and says, "As you know, your late uncle left a very unusual will." Have the heirs lined up on either end of a rope for a tug-of-war and let the lawyer utter his line. Have

"Robert came into a large inheritance as a child."

him say it at sea as he stands on the deck of one of two battleships, or in a battlefield situation with two tanks or two cannons.

Sometimes switches can work by isolating one element in a cartoon from everything else and thinking about how many parallel situations can be drawn from that one element. Props work well this way. Earlier we talked about props in an expansive way as stimuli to many different kinds of ideas. Here, we want to illustrate a narrower, but equally effective, use of props.

Take a different but equally hoary cartoon premise. A male bather stands on a beach and holds a conch shell—a prop—to his ear. In real life, he hears "the sound of the sea." How many other sounds can be switched into the situation? He hears his boss nag him: "Dammit, Perkins, you good-for-nothing goldbricker, get back to work!" He hears a disk jockey:

"And now here's a favorite of mine, 'By the Sea, by the Beautiful Sea.'" He hears a commercial for public radio: "This Sound of the Sea was made possible by grants from . . ." He hears a sound bite prophesy: "The end is near! Details at eleven." He hears a proposition: "Want to come up into my shell and see my etchings?" He hears an idea for a cartoon: "How about exchanging the seashell prop for the little name tags people wear at conventions and other meetings?"

The ubiquitous name tags are a fine prop. We switched them from a convention to a different setting and generated this cartoon. Since one can obviously do legitimate switches from one's own cartoons as well as from those drawn by others, we got to thinking about new ways we might use that prop. We thought of a collection of ancient Greek gods atop Mount Olympus with tags on their lapels that say "Hi! I'm Zeus," "Hi! I'm Athena," and so on; a cocktail party of Christian saints, including one who is a young man with many arrows stuck through him and a name tag that says, "Hi! I'm Sebastian"; three ghosts confronting Scrooge, with tags that say "Hi! I'm the Ghost of Christmas Past [Present] [Future]"; seven loathsome looking creatures with tags for the Seven Deadly Sins: "Hi! I'm Gluttony," "Hi! I'm Lust," and on through the rest. There are undoubtedly many more.

Switches may also come off words or cliché phrases when we think about the setting in which they usually occur. This cartoon makes use of

"She can forgive Nixon, but she can't forgive me."

a particular political memory, but the operational word in it is "forgive." Keeping the setting in the marriage counselor's office, we might try to do switches on the notion of forgiveness. "She occasionally forgives, but she never forgets," the husband complains. "He can forgive everybody's trespasses except mine," the wife says. Take a different situation. Many cartoons have used the setting of an award banquet where someone toasts

"To a wonderful, amphibious being!"

"To a great lawyer!" or "To a fine doctor!" or even, in an expansive mode, "To a wonderful human being!" How about other kinds of beings? The cartoon practically begs for more switches. A lion to another: "To a great carnivorous being!" An angel to an angel: "To a great eternal being!" A witch to a witch: "To a great evil being!"

Abstracting a concept from a cartoon may also be a jumping-off place for a switch. Consider this cartoon. The concept here is a familiar one. When we "perform" in public, we assume the kind of physical appearance that people in our audience have come to expect from us, in this case, for flamingos, a one-legged stance. The concept could be switched by using other "performers," or other character types. Do monkeys read *War and Peace* or calculate quadratic equations when no one is around, but perform monkeylike antics when people come to the zoo? Do the faces on the famous Easter Island statues actually smile most of the time, but change to their traditional glum expressions when an anthropologist visits them? Does a flower close up its petals when it's alone, but open them so a doctor can put a thermometer in its "mouth"?

So far, we've been talking about more or less orderly switches from one idea to another. But sometimes—perhaps more often than not—switches go in directions that are disorderly and unpredictable but still productive. One of us saw a cartoon showing Christopher Columbus aboard one of his ships. As he sights land in the Americas, a sailor says something like, "Just think, Columbus! You'll have a whole continent named after you." Using the principle of opposites, the one of us asked how the indigenous peoples might have viewed Columbus's arrival. A cliché phrase leaped immediately to mind. He put it in the mouth of a man viewing Columbus's arrival from an island. "Well, there goes the neighborhood," the man says. The idea had already appeared in print, the one of us recalled, so he dumped it. But the principle of similarities came to his rescue. What was an equivalent to Columbus's arrival? He put the same line in the mouth of a space creature on a strange planet who viewed the arrival of earth people on a rocket ship. The switch worked and was original.

We have found that the process of switching from other cartoons is, paradoxically, both unpredictable and reliable. A particular cartoon may set off ideas one time, and not another. Or a cartoon that has provoked no associations on first glance may be rich in material later. But leafing through a collection of cartoons almost always produces some drawings that generate new ideas. Using other cartoons and switching them is also an economical way to generate concepts for funny drawings because a given switch is likely to lead to several more. One of our mentors in the business said, "You ought to be able to use any good idea at least four times."

Switching is the way to do that.

19
Seasonal Material

In *Love's Labour's Lost*, Shakespeare has a character say, "At Christmas I no more desire a rose than wish a snow in May's newfangled mirth; but like of each thing that in season grows." Experiences that are unique to a particular time of the year are a source of delight (and sometimes irritation) for everyone. But for cartoonists, the sensations, events, and activities that come with each season have a special meaning. They are a rich source of ideas for funny drawings.

However, cartoonists often must ignore Shakespeare's admonition about enjoying things in their proper time. The reason is simple. Most major magazines are laid out five or six months ahead of their scheduled publication date. To be timely with seasonal material a cartoonist must therefore think "out of season." In fact, the schedule for the submission of most such cartoon ideas is an almost exact inversion of the actual year. If it's October, a cartoonist should be thinking about drawings that refer to the Ides of March, St. Patrick's Day, and baseball spring training. If it's November, a humorous artist should be thinking about April Fool's Day, income tax forms, and the opening of the baseball season. Because of this anachronism, the creation of seasonal material is one of the great imaginative challenges of cartooning.

Picture a June day in New England, where both of us live. The lettuce in the garden is at the edible stage, gaggles of teachers are trying to control hordes of restless schoolchildren who know that summer vacation is in sight, and the Red Sox are winning. We, however, are not thinking about any of those subjects. We are thinking about December, when lettuce is available only in stores, when gaggles of teachers are trying to control hordes of restless schoolchildren who know that Christmas break is in sight, and when the Red Sox—who have, as usual, blown it in September—are a distant memory.

"Please, Edgar! Everyone's staring!"

Many topics come to mind when we think about December—the winter solstice, sleds, toboggans, ice skates, hockey, basketball, vacations in warmer climates. But probably—at least in an American setting—the richest set of December associations are those built around Christmas. The Christmas season and our images of it abound with sources for productive association.

Consider props. The first ones that come to mind are Christmas trees. Viewed literally, these evergreens suggest cartoons about buying a tree, getting a tree home in the car, decorating a tree. A variety of subordinate props—lights, tinsel, ornaments—go with those activities. Cartoons can be built around any of these situations and props, particularly if we insert an element of conflict about them, say an argument between a husband and wife about how to buy or decorate a tree.

But Christmas trees also conjure up other associations. An evergreen is supposed to be symbolic of the continuation of life even in the most bleak and lifeless part of the year. We might think about that from the tree's point of view. One tree says to another, "Why, thanks. And may I say that I think you too are a very classy symbol of the continuation of life even in the most bleak and lifeless part of the year?" Take another tack. Given the symbolism, what are we to make of plastic Christmas trees?

"Look dear!" says a man to his wife about one, "Here's a symbol of the continuation of life even in the most bleak and lifeless part of the year. And it's guaranteed not to shed needles." The needles might suggest a different way to think about a real tree. An elaborately decorated tree thinks about the people who decorated it: "They love me now. But in two weeks they'll be complaining about me shedding needles."

Cast your mind over a recent Christmas season, and you'll quickly come up with other props. Consider mistletoe. How does *it* feel? A vain man approaches a doorway hung with the plant. The mistletoe thinks, "Not *him* again!" Take stockings. Use the big and small contrast. Picture kids looking for the biggest possible stocking to hang. Imagine wreaths. A man holding a wreath only the size of a donut tells his family, "Fair warning. This year we're really scaling down on Christmas."

Christmas-related settings are an equally good source of ideas. There's the department store locale. It lends itself to many ideas about shopping until we're dropping, doing our part for the national consumer economy, worrying about how to pay the bills we've run up. Department stores also evoke the frequently used but still viable premise of the kid sitting on Santa's lap. "Before we begin," a precocious moppet says to the man in the red outfit, "a few words about malpractice suits." The family Christmas dinner, with its invitations to overeating and its renewal of ancient family feuds, is no less fruitful as a source for humor. "Well," says one family member to the others, "we've all stuffed ourselves to the gills and resurrected every miserable thing we've done to one another during the past twenty years. I

" 'Twas the night before Christmas . . ."
—Thomas Nast

guess it's time to go home." Other possible settings include the endless round of pre-Christmas receptions, the office Christmas party, the downtown streets filled with shoppers.

Christmas images are also full of characters and character types. First, of course, there's Santa. Obviously he's a man who needs advice from a qualified and fully certified nutritionist. Perhaps Mrs. Claus has put him on a low-cholesterol, low-fat, no-sugar diet. He may be glad to escape once a year to houses that always have milk and cookies waiting for him. Or, after endless plates of cookies and glasses of milk, perhaps he's delighted to find a fireplace with a martini pitcher beside it. Santa's employees—eight reindeer and uncounted elves—appear in many cartoons. Perhaps Mr. Claus is a terrible boss. A set of Santas sits across a negotiating table from a set of reindeer. Or a set of elves might picket Santa's workshop.

"Merry Old Santa Claus"
—Thomas Nast

Santa is also associated with props that may suggest cartoons. He wears a red suit and hat. Does he take them to the dry cleaners every

December 26? Think flying sleighs. Does Santa have to get clearance from air traffic controllers? Imagine chimneys. Santa may get stuck in one and decide he really *does* need to consult a nutritionist.

Go beyond Santa and his entourage to other character types. The little street-corner bands associated with the Salvation Army invite humor; perhaps the conductor of one of them imagines himself, dressed in a tuxedo, as the leader of a great symphony orchestra. Salespeople advising customers about Christmas gifts, bank tellers redeeming Christmas Club memberships, and people who send or receive Christmas cards are other possible Christmas character types.

And, of course, there are many clichés that go with Christmas. These days Santa probably uses a computer to help him keep track of who has been naughty and who has been nice. Or he may have decided that, in a world of relative values, those concepts are obsolete. The modern kid who sees Mommy kissing Santa Claus probably gets the whole scene on tape with his camcorder. The man who has invited his friends over to help him deck his halls may worry about whether he has adequate liability insurance. A judge dressed like Santa Claus may take a dim view of the activities of an errant mouse: "Definitely guilty of stirring on Christmas Eve. Thirty days, suspended, and one hundred hours of community service." A psychiatrist may reassure a troubled man: "Not to worry. This time of year, many of us have an irresistible urge to say 'Bah, Humbug!'" Cartoons built around any of these premises might produce, if not a hearty "ho, ho, ho" that makes a viewer shake like a bowl full of jelly, at least a small chuckle of Christmas cheer.

Once we've used basic associations with these premises, we can begin to mix and match them with sources of ideas that are not related to Christmas at all. Use unrelated settings: does Santa bask on a beach the day after Christmas? Use unrelated props: does Santa have to carry a pooper scooper for the reindeer? Use unrelated character types: does a lawyer promise to protect Santa against malpractice suits? Use unrelated animals: what kind of stockings might an elephant hang? Use unrelated fairy tales: do relatives of the enchanted frog who is now king complain because they get turkey, and not flies, for Christmas dinner? Use unrelated history: does a caveman carve a wreath instead of a wheel? Use unrelated literature: does Moby Dick find a brightly wrapped package with a little card on it that says, "Seasons greetings, with much love, (signed) Captain Ahab?" Use unrelated movies: did King Kong really climb the Empire State Building because he wanted to put a Christmas tree on top of it?

On the other hand, it also could be that King Kong climbed the

"If it's all the same to you, I'd rather have cash."

"I say Happy New Year and to hell with it!"

Empire State Building so he could get a better view of the big ball in Times Square as it falls to mark midnight on New Year's Eve. With that association, we might move to another holiday that cartoonists must think about in June or July. Once more, to stimulate our thinking, we have props—noisemakers, funny hats, and champagne corks—settings—Times Square, a party at a nightclub—verbal clichés—New Year's resolutions, "Auld Lang Syne"—and visual cliché characters—Father Time and Baby New Year.

New Year's Eve over, we can look forward to another entire year of seasonal events, each of which will generate many cartoon ideas. January brings endless play-off games and finally the Super Bowl; February gives us Valentine's Day, Groundhog Day, and an occasional leap year; May offers Mother's Day and flowers; July provides Independence Day and vacations, September furnishes Labor Day and school opening. The mere mention of any of these seasonal events is likely to conjure up a set of props, characters, settings, and clichés. But if memory alone isn't enough, consult *Chase's Annual Events*, which lists observances and events for every day of the year, or a seasonal comedy reference work like Gag

"Honey! You remembered!"

Recap Publications' *Comedy Calendar Guide* (see Bibliography). You'll find that every season provides a rich array of gifts in the form of funny visual ideas. And, unlike Shakespeare's character, you may find that you enjoy thinking about snow in May or roses at Christmas. After all, one of the surest routes to humor is incongruity.

"I'm Kenneth H. Rydell, of 176 East Sixty-third Street, and I don't have time for the waiting game."

III
Developing and Polishing Funny Ideas

Generating ideas is one step—probably the most demanding step—in the creation of visual humor. But there are other steps along the route from an idea to a finished drawing. In this section, we'll talk about how to take ideas generated by using the techniques we've discussed and convert them into full-fledged comic pictures. We'll first discuss how a raw idea can be polished into a finished concept. Then we'll talk about polishing captions that can work with the concept. We'll also discuss ways in which ideas can be polished to make them appeal to particular audiences. Finally, we'll give an example of how we "put it all together" in an actual idea-creating session.

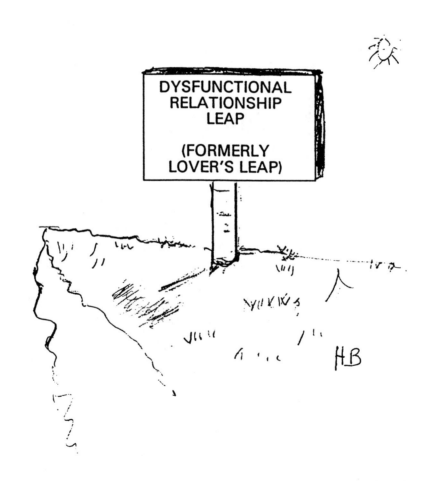

20
Developing and Polishing
a Concept

Many—perhaps most—ideas for successful cartoons first emerge in rough form. After associations that involve some or many of the techniques we've outlined, a notion emerges that has obvious humorous potential. But the concept is unformed, primitive. We must—like a jeweler with a raw gem—take the basic material and polish it.

Sometimes polishing a concept is relatively simple. An idea may, for example, begin with a funny picture that simply needs a humorous line to go with it. As an example, start with a visual cliché: a man and a woman wait, hand in hand, on the edge of Lover's Leap. Add a prop: he wears a parachute. The idea is amusing, but it's not quite there as a full-fledged cartoon. It needs a caption.

Who speaks? The woman is the one who is surprised at the situation, so she should utter the line. What does she say? She could comment about the parachute: "I knew there was a reason you bought that damn parachute, Henry." That caption is not funny because the line is too obvious; it simply repeats the premise. How can the concept be improved with a better line?

Probably the best way to polish the concept is to try to feel our way into the woman's state of mind. She's hurt and angry. When we're angry at someone, often we don't limit ourselves to attacking the person for what he or she has actually done to us. We generalize about all those things we dislike about the person. So she may say something nasty about his entire personality: "You always were a coward, weren't you, Henry?"

That's funnier than the first line, but it's still not really punchy. Are there emotions that are even more profound than her resentment about his cowardice? She's deeply hurt and angry because he is obviously not taking her, or their relationship, seriously. The deeper emotion and the words *relationship* and *seriously* suggest a funny line: she says, "You never were serious about our relationship, were you, Henry?" And we have a polished cartoon idea.

Take the opposite of a picture without a caption. Our associations generate a line that has comic potential, but will only work with an appropriate picture. Let's use words from a song. (Song lyrics and titles are really a specialized kind of cliché. Because so many of us have little snippets from popular music lodged somewhere in our minds, they are

"I like a Gershwin tune. How about you?"

frequently useful in cartooning.) Once we found a Cole Porter line running through our heads: "I like a Gershwin tune. How about you?" It seemed to invite a funny picture.

Who might utter the words to make them humorous? Our first notion was to put the lyrics in the mouth of an opera singer who wore an elaborate Wagnerian costume. But, in fact, Gershwin wrote operatic music, so that picture idea was a little—pardon the expression—flat. When we put the words in the mouth of a member of a funky, weird-looking rock band, they become a little funnier. Having a caveman who plays primitive wood and bone instruments utter the sentence was an additional improvement. But both ideas seemed too literal; they simply transferred the line from one human music maker to another. People think of some animals as making music too. That seemed a more promising avenue to explore. What animal could we use? Wolves howling at the moon were one possibility. So were canaries and parrots. But there is a classic visual cliché about animals who make music. Putting the line with that picture produced the cartoon opposite.

Most often, polishing a concept is not as simple as these first examples suggest. Polishing usually requires that we take a rough—even vague—idea and explore as many of its ramifications as we can until one emerges that maximizes its comic potential. The process might, for example, begin with a common prop. We'll choose automobiles. Nowadays, automobiles are our major means of transportation. Because they cause both pleasure and irritation, autos are a source of conflict, and so are a good basis for cartoons.

Autos invite the use of the principle of similarity. What's akin to automobiles? A century ago, horses were the main means of transportation. Horses, then, are in this way similar to autos. The principle inherent in most historical cartoons—anachronism—provides the beginning of a cartoon concept. What if some of the same irritating things that now befall people who use automobiles happened to people who relied on horses for transportation?

There are many irritating aspects of automobile ownership. Auto salespeople try to sell customers a lemon. Horse traders who were swindlers were a staple of nineteenth-century humor, but they aren't widely recognizable as a funny premise now. Think of automobile repair-

Harper's Weekly, October 16, 1886

people. The equivalent for horses are veterinarians. This drawing, which lampooned the S.P.C.A., was amusing to some people in the nineteenth century, but horse doctors are too unfamiliar to be funny to many people today. Think about traffic jams. Now we're getting closer to a viable idea. Is it possible to draw a picture of a "horse jam"? Probably not, or at least not in a way that would make sense to a contemporary viewer.

How about parking tickets? There, finally, is an idea that feels usable. What if "parked" horses were given parking tickets? A captionless cartoon might show a whole row of horses tied to a hitching post, each of them with a parking ticket attached to its saddle or bridle. That's probably a funny enough cartoon idea in itself. Can we make the idea even stronger? Picture the setting with which many of us associate horses and a hitching post: the Wild West. We might simply put a cowboy in the picture and have him emerge from a saloon to view the ticket his horse has received. That polishes the cartoon by adding a human character who sees the anachronism. But we can also add one other clichéd visual image from the Wild West to make an even stronger picture. Make the owner of one of the horses a bank robber. A bandana over his mouth, his six-guns blazing, the robber emerges from a bank and finds a cop—or perhaps a sheriff—putting a parking ticket on his horse. The idea is both original and funny.

That cartoon concept involved polishing by associating around one parallel—horses and cars. Often polishing is more complex. A raw idea must be developed by using many cartoon elements: say a visual cliché, a character type, a setting, and a similarity.

Start with a visual cliché: a devil. Think of him as a character type—a professional. His profession? Evil, of course. Some people are in the auto repair business, some are in the insurance business, some are in the men's underwear business. He's in the evil business. It's a funny notion.

Add some other visual elements to flesh out the character. Dress our devil like a regular businessman. He wears a suit and a tie. Put him in a setting. He's behind a desk in a big, plush business office. He now looks much like a regular businessman.

Think of our devil as *really* similar to a regular businessman. Imagine his background, his personality, his emotions. Like many businessmen, he's proud of his achievements. He feels he has worked hard to get where he is. How *did* he get where he is? Perhaps he began with a small business, which then grew larger. Now we're getting close to a usable cartoon idea. How did his business begin? Suppose that initially he was an amateur evildoer. He found he was so good at it that he decided he'd turn professional. Give our devil someone to talk to—say a reporter. (In this case, the reporter is really a prop.) The devil says, "Well, Ed, when I was just a kid and starting out doing evil, it was only a hobby. I had no idea, of course, that eventually I'd be heading up a multinational corporation."

Polishing the notion about the devil as a businessman led to one finished cartoon concept. If we're lucky, sometimes we can find several ways to polish a raw idea. In effect, polishing becomes a form of switching that can produce a number of usable picture concepts from a single premise.

To illustrate, let's begin with a durable, even hoary, cartoon premise that we discussed earlier: Noah's ark. Thinking around the ark tale, we come to the final scene. The dove arrives back with the olive branch. The

dove's arrival is a monumental historical moment. Consider monumental historical moments today. What happens when they occur? In our era of instant communication, often enough there are television crews on the scene to record the event. Put a TV crew on the ark to broadcast the dove's arrival. The idea is funny. It can be polished in several ways.

We might take the notion we used when we talked about switching: people "put on" an expression when they know they're being watched. Invert the idea. Noah knows this is an important event, so he *wants* to be watched. Make a multipanel drawing. The dove arrives. Noah motions for it to go away. (This creates suspense in the viewer; why has Noah done this?) Noah talks on the phone. A TV crew arrives on the deck of the ark. Smiling broadly, Noah watches as the dove lands for a second time, its arrival now photographically recorded for posterity.

Another way to polish the idea is to add a caption. The TV crew is on the ark. Who talks? Try an animal observing the scene. One says to his partner, about Noah, "Of course when I first heard about the trip, I thought the old geezer was just a crackpot." Try Noah. He speaks directly to the TV audience, like a modern-day politician. "Never have so few done so much for so many," he says, paraphrasing a famous twentieth-century pol. The dove might also speak. This event represents its lifetime quota of fifteen (or five) minutes of fame. It wants to make the most of them. Think of award ceremonies, like Oscar night. The dove says something like, "I'd like to thank all those who made this moment possible: Noah, who entrusted me with this important mission, all doves everywhere who have provided role models and inspiration, the many, many other animals who believed in me, and last, but certainly not least, my wonderful mother, who first taught me to fly."

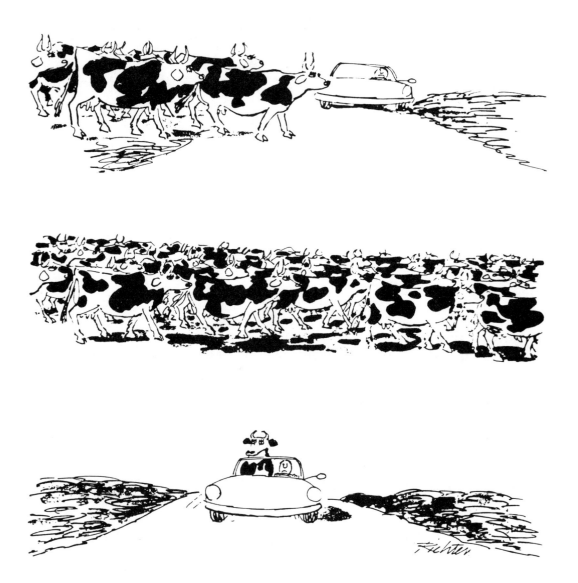

We've taken several raw ideas and illustrated ways they can be successfully polished into finished concepts. But before we leave the subject, it's necessary to insert an important caveat about the process. Like polishing gems, polishing ideas is an unpredictable process. A substantial amount of work may produce a concept with only a dim luster. It's our experience that there's a certain point in the polishing process when it becomes clear that an idea is simply not, at least at the moment, going to turn into a jewel. In that case, it's probably best to abandon the notion and turn to some other raw material.

But it's also our experience that if the idea has real potential, it will continue to be polished in that mysterious place below the surface of our minds where creation takes place. We've had raw ideas, abandoned at one idea-creating session, reemerge hours, days, or even weeks later in finished form. So we've learned never totally to abandon an idea that seems promising. We may jot it down in crude form, or push it into the recesses of memory. If the notion was good in the first place, it will eventually come back in a workable version.

For example, as we write this, we have been musing for some time about a report one of us heard on a TV show that stated that cows belch methane. So far, no viable cow and methane cartoon has emerged from this musing. However, we're confident that sometime, some day, thousands of readers will be howling —and taking in gasps of cow-produced methane—at a drawing based on the premise. We're giving our unconscious minds time to ruminate on the idea.

21
Developing and Polishing Captions

Once a concept has been polished until it makes maximum use of its latent humorous potential, there is an additional level of refining that needs to be done. If the cartoon involves a caption, the words must also be polished to give the concept its most powerful realization. We have seen many otherwise viable cartoon concepts fail because the artist has not taken the time or effort to polish a drawing's caption.

Like a good cook, a cartoonist who is writing a caption must search for exactly the right mixture of ingredients to make a creation savory. Most beginning cartoonists err by overstuffing their captions. Bloated with unnecessary words, the lines become flat and flavorless. There used to be an unwritten rule in the cartooning business that a caption should run no more than eight words. That maxim should be taken with a grain of salt (or more, if the recipe calls for it). Still, eight to twelve or fifteen words is not a bad goal to set for captions. After all, as some writer or other once observed, brevity *is* the soul of wit.

It's also possible, though, to err in the opposite direction: to squeeze a caption by eliminating necessary words until it becomes juiceless. The ancient Greeks—in life, if not necessarily in cooking or caption writing—supposedly worshiped the golden mean. When cartoonists write captions, they should pay homage to the same ideal.

Cartoonists can learn a good deal about this golden mean by observing the ways fiction writers create dialogue. In successful novels, short stories, plays, and films, dialogue *seems* to sound like real conversation. But in fact, fictional dialogue is carefully constructed to give an abbreviated *illusion* of reality.

Imagine a woman who returns to her spouse after a hard day's work. She wants to tell him about a funny experience she had on the way home. Here are three versions of the way she might begin her tale:

1. "Ha, ha, ha. Hey, Walt," Louise said. "You know . . . um . . . a really funny . . . er . . . actually, a hilarious thing happened . . . you know . . . happened today when I was going . . . running, in fact . . . down Pearl Street. Right there where Pearl meets Apple Way . . . um . . . where the Murrays used to live. Anyway . . . you know . . . you wouldn't believe it, but . . . ha, ha, ha . . . I can hardly tell it, it was so funny . . ."

2. "As I walked down Pearl Street today, I observed something humorous," Louise said.

3. "Hey, Walt!" Louise said. "You wouldn't believe the funny thing that happened today on Pearl Street."

The first version is the way the conversation would probably go in real life. When people actually talk, they sputter, "um" and "er," insert irrelevant information, repeat themselves, and just plain blither. When we listen, we (mostly) tune out the hesitations and irrelevancies and get the message. But in print, "real" conversation is dreadfully dull.

The second version is the content of the conversation reduced to its minimum. It accurately conveys its message. But the sentence is too brief. And it sounds stuffy and stilted. People don't often really talk that way. Unless you're establishing a stuffy and stilted character, the sentence doesn't work as printed conversation.

The third version is the way a fiction writer might handle this piece of dialogue. The structure of the sentence lets us know that Louise is excited and amused. The diction is colloquial enough to give an illusion of real conversation. People *do* talk that way. But the sentence has been drastically cut from its real-life version. Not only have the hesitations and nonspeech usages of real language—the "ums," "ers," and "you knows"—been pruned, but bits of extraneous data that add nothing to the sentence's meaning, like the exact location of the incident, have also been eliminated. In short, the third version is both colloquial and economical. A reader who comes upon it is likely to want to read on to find out what was funny.

Like fiction writers, cartoonists who write dialogue must find a balance between colloquial sound and economy of language. And they

"Say something funny, even if it's contrived."

must do something more. They must also arrange the sentences in a caption so they produce a laugh.

The challenge of caption writing, then, is to produce lines that are conversational, economical, *and* funny.

Let's follow a caption from an initial concept through to a polished version. Take a cartoon cliché scene. The boss has called in our character, Hopeless Hartman, and fired him. Poor Hopeless, of course, is desperate. He wants to protest. What argument might he use? He might say, "What about my wife and kids?" (Even that sentence is a pared-down version of real-life talk. In the actual situation, Hopeless would probably "um" and "er" in helpless confusion for quite a while.) "What about my wife and kids?" might work in serious fiction, but it's not funny. Still, the line provides a beginning point for a sentence or sentences that can be made to work as a caption.

We can start to polish the line by changing the speaker. It's a rule in caption writing that a reply is usually funnier than a question. We suspect that this is because the reader gets a little extra sense of accomplishment by mentally supplying the initial, unstated, question. Whether or not that's true, a caption in the form of a reply gives a cartoon a sense of verbal motion that adds to its impact. So let's use a reply. Hopeless has said, "What about my wife and kids?" In the caption, the boss says, "I'm still

going to fire you, Hartman. The question of what happens to your family is of no concern to me."

That caption is not yet funny. It's wordy, awkward, and stilted. But we're moving toward a workable line. Carry the idea one step further. Suppose Hopeless, in a confused effort to bolster his sagging self-esteem, tells the boss how his family feels about him. "But my wife and kids think I'm wonderful," he says. Now we're closer to a funny line. There's something painfully absurd about the way Hopeless inserts this irrelevant information into the very serious situation. Again, make the caption the boss's reply. The boss says, "I'm still going to fire you, Hartman, no matter whether your wife and kids think you're wonderful or not." That's a funny *idea* for a line. We can turn it into an actual funny line by polishing it further.

One basic rule for humor writing of all kinds is that the punchy, surprising words in a sentence should be placed as near to the end of the sentence as possible. What's the punch, the surprise, here? Hartman has been fired. The reader won't know that until he or she reads the caption. Reverse the order of the sentence so the punch is closer to the end: "Whether your wife and kids think you're wonderful or not, Hartman, I'm still going to fire you." That's a better caption. But it's too long, and there is not a powerful enough buildup toward the surprise ending to make the surprise really funny.

Can the words about the firing be cut? How about simply, "you're still fired"? Now the surprise word is the last word in the sentence: "Whether your wife and kids think you're wonderful or not, Hartman, you're still fired."

We're getting close to a good caption, but it's still too wordy and the buildup is still weak. How can we repair the first part of the sentence? Maybe we can make the boss really sardonic. If he says, "I don't doubt for a moment that your wife and kids . . ." No. Let's make it even more brief: "I'm sure your wife and kids *do* think you're wonderful, Hartman. . . ." That's better. And it suggests an additional way to polish a caption: separate the punchy, surprising line from any others and make it a separate sentence. We'll give the line about Hartman being fired its own sentence.

The caption now reads: "I'm sure your wife and kids *do* think you're wonderful, Hartman. But you're still fired."

There! The caption has been pruned. Fewer words do the same job.

The punch line has been separated from the rest of the caption and the critical surprise word comes at the end. The sentence also sounds more conversational than previous versions.

Probably the caption is workable in that form. But is it possible to breathe even more life into the sentences? Read the caption slowly out loud, word by word. Are there weak words? *Wonderful* is weak. How about something at once more colloquial and more punchy? *Terrific* is better. *Super* is even better, more colloquial. What goes beyond super? How about "one hell of a human being"? "One hell of a human being" has the same meaning as *wonderful, terrific,* or *super.* But the phrase adds an additional intrinsic funny element to the caption because it is slangy and also slightly pretentious and so, in a droll way, amusing in itself.

The boss now says, "I'm sure your wife and kids *do* think you're one hell of a human being, Hartman. But you're still fired." We have a very strong caption.

Note that in this new version we actually added five words when we substituted "one hell of a human being" for *wonderful.* But, by slightly sacrificing economy, we have added both to the conversational quality and the humorous weight of the line.

While occasionally a full-blown, polished caption may spring to mind simultaneously with a cartoon concept, often when we write captions we

"Before I begin, I should warn you that in my quest for the truth and my relentless war against corruption I will now and then split an infinitive and end an occasional sentence with a preposition."

mentally go through a refining process much like the one just illustrated. Sometimes the process demands only a change in a single word; sometimes it demands a more complete revision like the one above. With experience, it has become more likely that the first caption that occurs to us will be closer to the optimal line.

But the refining process, quick or slow, conscious or unconscious, always follows much the same route. We think about the order of the words in the sentences and rearrange them to put the punch at the end. We scrutinize the caption and ask about each word, "Is it necessary?" and "Is it the strongest word possible?" And finally, sometimes we read the caption aloud to determine whether it gives an illusion of conversation. Often our ears will hear phony or awkward phrases that we miss on the printed page.

At last—if we're lucky—we settle back to enjoy a caption line that so well captures the golden mean that it would even have made Socrates laugh.

22
Creating Cartoons
for Specialized Audiences

Consider these three cartoon ideas:

1. A middle-aged woman says to a man in his twenties, "Even if I am your Mom, Wally, I don't need any more insurance."

2. A husband is opening a champagne bottle. His wife says to a friend, "He just figured out a way to get a major energy source from a simple mixture of soybeans and alfalfa."

3. First panel: two men meet and shake hands. Man A gets a shock from a little buzzer held in the hand of man B. Second panel: man B squirts man A with water from a fake flower on his lapel. Third panel: the two go off, each with an arm around the other's shoulder, laughing.

It's unlikely that any of these notions sent you rolling on the floor in uncontrollable spasms of laughter. But there are people from whom these drawings might elicit at least a chuckle, and perhaps even a full-fledged laugh.

Like beauty and political attractiveness, humor is very much in the mind of the beholder. What's ho-ho for the goose may be ho-hum for the gander. Many factors that make different people laugh at different things are individual and idiosyncratic. Anyone who has been in the humor business for any length of time has met people who just don't get his or her jokes. Probably every humor professional also has a mental list of

"Some friends of the farmer here to see you, sir."

other humorists whose humor he or she just doesn't get. Anyone who tries to create humor that will appeal to everyone is bound to fail.

It is possible, however, to create ideas designed to produce a laugh from people who belong to a particular group. Because of their shared background and interests, members of a group will find some things funny that readers in a more general audience will not. From time to time, many of us are asked to produce concepts of this kind. We have, for example, created ideas for political movements, theatrical troupes, parents' groups and other organizations, and for many trade journals that are oriented to specific professions.

In the cartooning business, such notions are known as *slanted* ideas—the slant being the reorientation of an idea that inclines a cartoon toward a particular audience. In general, the best way to create cartoon ideas is to let your mind range as widely as possible, collect whatever notions emerge, draw them, and then decide who might find them funny. But it's also useful to know how to develop slanted material like the three ideas above.

Not to keep you in suspense. The three ideas are slanted, respectively, to 1) insurance salespeople, 2) farmers, 3) owners of novelty and joke shops.

These are examples of what are called "tight" slants. The audience for each type of cartoon is relatively small. We'll return to the subject of tight slants in a minute. Much slanted material, though, is oriented to fairly large subgroups within the general cartoon-viewing audience. If you read through several issues of a few major publications, you'll begin to get an idea of the kind of slant each one uses for its readers. The difference

between the cartoons the magazines use is often not so much in the setting or characters as it is in the nature of the caption or humorous situation. Frequently, in fact, the same picture can be oriented to one or another magazine simply by altering the caption to fit the interests of the magazine's readers.

For example, imagine a drawing. It is the middle of the night. A man, a startled and worried expression on his face, sits bolt upright in bed. The woman in bed beside him speaks the caption. Here are four lines she might utter, each oriented to a different publication.

The New Yorker: "No, I haven't heard rumors about someone planning a leveraged buyout of our marriage. Now go back to sleep."

Playboy: "What do you mean, 'There'll be hell to pay if my wife finds out'? I *am* your wife."

Cosmopolitan: "Of course I'll respect you in the morning."

The National Enquirer: "I *do* forgive you for not taking out the garbage. Now go back to sleep."

Each caption fits the readers of the particular magazine: the upscale audience of *The New Yorker*, often concerned with matters of business; the overwhelmingly male audience of *Playboy*, for whom issues about sexual prowess and infidelity are presumably worrisome; the predominantly female readers of *Cosmopolitan*, who will appreciate the inversion of the traditional cliché about women; the family-oriented audience of the

National Enquirer, who may laugh at the familiar domestic reference. It is unlikely that these publications would print any of the cartoons save the one oriented to their readers.

If one is actually marketing cartoons to magazines with large readerships, finding drawings that match a magazine's slant is often a matter of selecting cartoons from those already drawn (or deciding that the kind of humor one produces simply doesn't match a given magazine's needs). With tight slants for a narrow audience, though, it's possible to steer your mind into channels where the generation of ideas with an appeal to specific groups of people is more likely.

The basic ingredients for tightly slanted ideas are the props, settings, characters, words, visual and verbal clichés, and other devices we have talked about. The trick in slanting is to view those ingredients from the point of view of the people you're trying to amuse.

As an example, let's say our target audience is elementary school teachers. If we think back to our own experience in elementary school, it's easy to come up with ingredients for cartoons. A small movement away from our own experience can make those ingredients funny for teachers.

We can start with props. Imagine homework. From our point of view as students, homework meant struggling to write about something that was new to us; our problem with homework was comprehension. From a teacher's point of view, homework means struggling to read huge numbers of papers about something that is all too familiar; a teacher's problem with homework is repetition. As we all know, anything that is endlessly repeated can turn our minds to mush. Picture a schoolyard. A teacher goes swinging from tree to tree like an ape, pieces of paper trailing behind him. Another teacher says: "He just graded 113 papers about the theory of evolution."

Take another common prop we all remember from our school years: the blackboard, with the alphabet written in block letters above it. The material on the blackboard and the alphabet included lessons we had to learn. But suppose the teacher wants to teach us something beyond what's

already there. Add something to the alphabet. It now reads
A B C D E F G H I J I M M Y, P U T Y O U R G U M
I N T H E W A S T E B A S K E T! K L M N O P Q
R S T U V W X Y Z.

Or try report cards. They're the bane of a student's existence, but
they're also one of the banes of a teacher's existence. Preparing report
cards—particularly the newer forms, which often require extensive comments in addition to letter grades—eats up hours of a teacher's time and
ergs of his or her energy. Put a teacher on a psychiatrist's couch. The
shrink says, "Not to worry, Miss Burbank. Many teachers go into severe
depression when report card time comes around."

School settings can also stimulate ideas. We probably remember our
classrooms, the playground, perhaps the school gym or auditorium. Any
of them can work as a setting for a teacher-oriented cartoon if it is looked
at from a teacher's point of view. For us as kids, for example, playgrounds
meant relief from classroom demands. For teachers they mean trying to
keep a group of boisterous—and perhaps quarrelsome—children in some
kind of minimal order. ("I can't wait until recess is over," one teacher says
to another.) For a student, a program in the school auditorium might
mean savoring a moment in the limelight. For a teacher, it might mean
confronting an angry parent who wonders why little Betsy didn't get the
starring role in the school's annual reenactment of the signing of the
Declaration of Independence. Teachers also work in settings that students
seldom see. What goes on in the teacher's lounge? In the principal's
office? At a PTA or school board meeting? Any of these settings can
generate ideas.

Clichés—both visual and verbal—abound in educational settings. Try
"an apple for the teacher." What if the teacher is allergic to apples?
Perhaps a child brings something else to the teacher—say a pear, or the
broccoli the child refused to eat at dinner the night before, or an Apple
computer. Maybe an enterprising kid gets a monopoly on the apple-

delivery business at his
school, and a teacher has to
deal with that. Go further
afield. Is the real story about
the Garden of Eden that the
serpent was trying to get a
good grade from Eve? For
another cliché, think about
essays on "what I did during
my summer vacation." What
did the *teacher* do during
summer vacation? Try to supplement his or her modest salary by selling

"This has been quite a year for Zobrowsky—a hundred and twenty-nine receptions, sixteen touchdowns, a B-plus in English, a B in philosophy, an A in political science, and a B-minus in French."

encyclopedias? Finish grading the other 113 papers on evolution? "Those who can, do; those who can't, teach," goes the saying. Where does that leave professors in the schools of education, who teach teachers?

Any number of nursery rhymes can also be fodder for teacher-oriented ideas. Did the teacher despair because the little lamb was a first-rate student, but Mary was a hopeless underachiever? Perhaps Tweedledum and Tweedledee kept copying one another's homework. After her encounter with the wolf, Little Red Riding Hood might have brought some interesting items to present at "show and tell" time.

Schools and school settings are also full of jargon. Perhaps because teachers basically make their living by talking, they can laugh at pretentiousness in language. Words like *innovative*—as applied to curricula, teaching methods, or almost anything else—*multicultural, relevant, sex education, in-service training*, and *accountability* are perfect examples of jargon that can form the basis for humor that will appeal to teachers. If you can come up with an innovative and multicultural cartoon idea that is relevant to sex education and can be taught to faculty during in-service training programs, you can certainly be held accountable for a good many laughs from teachers.

Seeing a subject from inside the mind of a member of a group like teachers also means avoiding subjects that members of the group will *not* find funny. Educators are unlikely to laugh at cartoons about cruel or sadistic teachers, even though we may have all experienced them and such cartoons may appeal to other people. Similarly, cartoons about in-

"It's publish or perish, and he hasn't published."

George Cruikshank

competent doctors, or about doctors charging outrageous fees, while common in general-circulation magazines, are not funny to physicians. Dentists in general don't find cartoons about excruciating dental pain laughable, lawyers don't chortle at ideas that involve ambulance-chasing or unscrupulous legal tactics, and construction engineers find nothing amusing about drawings involving buildings made from inferior materials.

As you begin to create tightly slanted ideas, it's probably best to start with the fields with which you are most familiar. These may include not only your own work or profession, but also your hobbies, your avocations, your fascinations. If you're an architecture buff, an avid skier, a golf nut, a fanatic bowler, a stamp collector, an amateur musician, a devoted poker player, you're on the way to tightly slanted material. Eventually, as your "gag sense" develops, you'll probably be able to generate ideas that deal

with areas about which you have less knowledge. Listening to friends or family members talk about their interests is a good way to begin to broaden your scope.

Eventually, though, you may reach a limit. Some years ago, one of us was asked to produce twenty ideas that would seem funny to professional turkey growers. He worked at the project for a long time. But all he could think about were memories of three years during his childhood when he lived in a house that was downwind from a turkey farm. Finally—despite the wound to his professional self-esteem—he gave up on the assignment. Presumably some other creative person, less encumbered by Proustian memories, generated the ideas, and the magazine that catered to turkey growers gobble-gobbled them up.

23
Putting It All Together:
A Sample Idea-Creating Session

Where to start night. Went to a play— *Cymbeline*. Not one of his greatest. today? Up late last Shakespeare's Very long too. Twenty zillion plots, all tied up too neatly at the end. To a modern taste, it seems melodramatic. Melodrama. Start there. An image of an old-time mustachioed villain tying the hapless heroine to a railroad track. What would be a modern-day equivalent? Tying her to a Commuter Rail track. She'd probably languish there for days before a train came. Won't work as a cartoon.

Think about the villain himself. What does he look like? Long flowing cape. Evil leer. What does he do for a living? Tie maidens to railroad tracks? Too specific. Generalize. His trade is villainy. Where would he get a job? Lots of villainy in contemporary corporate settings, though it goes under the name "white-collar crime." Suppose he thinks his villainy qualifies him for a job. He's applying for a position. Put him with a personnel officer. What does he say? "My main qualification is unparalleled villainy." Flat line. A response is funnier. Put a line in the mouth of the personnel officer. The personnel officer says: "Do you have any qualifications other than unparalleled villainy?" Idea number one. Write it down.

"Do you have any other qualifications?"

Melodrama. Melodramas were popular in the era just after the Civil War. Civil War. *Gone with the Wind.* "Frankly, Scarlett, I don't give a damn." Civil War. Abraham Lincoln. Lincoln went to a play the night he was assassinated. Maybe it was a melodrama. Old joke: "Other than that, Mrs. Lincoln, how did you like the play?" Grisly. Need happy associations with Lincoln. A visual image. Tall and thin. High hat. Beard. Could give him a different kind of facial hair—maybe a Salvador Dalí mustache, twirled out long and thin? Somebody did a cartoon about that, can't remember who. Trivia: Lincoln's dog was named Jip. So what? Other Lincoln associations. Rail splitting. Log cabins.

Log cabins. Syrup. Syrup and beards create a mess. Did Lincoln ever get syrup stuck in his beard? Syrup. Spigots stuck into maple trees to get sap for syrup. Had French toast for breakfast this morning. Used Grade A maple syrup. Suppose the spigots on the maple trees were rated? Put labels on them, like the labels on the spigots at filling stations: Grade A and Grade B or Regular and Super. Not very funny. Go with gasoline stations. Auto repairmen. A visual image of a guy standing beside his car. The repairman tells him something. What? Personalize the car. What's its problem? What kind of problems do *people* have these days? Jargon: they lack self-esteem. Maybe that's the car's problem. Auto mechanic tells owner, about car: "The boys think its basic problem is low self-esteem." Idea number two. Write it down.

What a pretentious phrase, "self-esteem"! Did Lincoln have a problem with self-esteem? Probably. Did Lincoln's dog, Jip, have a problem with self-esteem? Funny notion. What can the dog say to Lincoln? "I have self-esteem problems." Flat. Forget it. Still, a good idea. Write down "dogs and self-esteem," come back to it.

"I wish they would make up their minds. One day I'm 'good boy,' the next day I'm 'bad boy.'"

Look out the window. Brick sidewalks down below. Reminds me of brick sidewalks on colonial American streets. Fire hydrant at the end of the block. Did they have fire hydrants for dogs on colonial streets? Not likely. Maybe colonial dogs had self-esteem problems too. Imagine a colonial street. Who's walking down it? A town crier. "Ten o'clock, and all's well." All's well with what? His self-esteem. Write down: Line for colonial town crier: "Ten o'clock and all's well with my self-esteem." Idea number three.

There's grass growing up between the bricks on our sidewalk. Have to get at it one of these days, root it out. Grass. "The grass is always greener on the other side of the fence." Does that mean that the grass on the other side of the fence has higher self-esteem than the grass over here? Cows eat grass. Do cows who eat grass that has high self-esteem give milk

that's high in self-esteem content? "Waiting until the cows come home."
Cows. What would cause the cows who were coming home to have *low*
self-esteem? How about nondairy creamers for coffee? One cow says to
another, "Bad news. More nondairy creamers are in the offing." Idea
number four.

I'm losing my self-esteem by sticking with one premise. Go further
afield. Fields. Back to cows. Bulls. "That's no bull," we say. A euphemism
for "That's no bullshit." What do bulls say when they want to indicate

The cat is meowing because it thinks it's time to be fed. Has anybody
ever met a cat with low self-esteem? Impossible. Cats never have a moment
of self-doubt. Maybe a supercilious cat gives advice to a dog: "Basically,
like most dogs, your problem is low self-esteem." Not quite there as a
cartoon caption line yet. Write down "cats/dogs and self-esteem," come
back to it.

I'm losing my self-esteem by sticking with one premise. Go further
afield. Fields. Back to cows. Bulls. "That's no bull," we say. A euphemism
for "That's no bullshit." What do bulls say when they want to indicate

*"Who can say? I suppose I'm as happy as my portfolio
will allow me to be."*

something is serious, "That's no peopleshit"? No cartoon idea there. Bulls.
Bull markets. Bulls and bears. Bulls sit on one side of a negotiating table,
bears on the other. Not really funny. Bulls and bears pull on opposite

ends of a rope in a tug-of-war. Might work as a political cartoon, with the right caption. Bullish or bearish about the economy. Brokers are supposed to be one or the other. What if they're inconsistent? What's the broker's home life like? Wife says to friend, about stockbroker husband, "Edgar is bullish about everything except our marriage." Idea number six.

Marriage. What was Ambrose Bierce's definition? Look it up. "*Marriage*, n., a community consisting of a master, a mistress, and two slaves, making in all, two." Too mordant for my mood today. Think about twosomes. Famous pairs. Tristan and Iseult. Romeo and Juliet. Adam and Eve. Did the snake do his evil deed because he had a problem with self-

esteem? Twosomes. Tea for two. A couple at a table in a restaurant. Romantic setting. A strolling violin player. What other instrument might the strolling musician play. A flute? A sousaphone! Funny. What does one of the couple say about it? "Don't knock it until you've tried it." Doesn't work. Keep it in the back of your mind. There's got to be a funny caption about a strolling sousaphone player.

Sousaphones. Marching bands. *The Music Man.* "Seventy-six trombones . . ." Parades. Fourth of July celebrations. Politicians orating. Politicians on the campaign trail. Promises made to be broken. Trying to be all things to all people. Look at it from the point of view of the politician. He's on the podium, trying to ingratiate himself with the voters. He starts,

*"I should like to depart from my prepared text and speak
as a human being."*

"My fellow citizens . . ." My fellow citizens of what? He doesn't know
where he is. He says, "My fellow citizens of (Insert Name of Town)!" Idea
number seven.

The cat is getting more insistent about getting its food. Food. Food
chain. Where does cat food fit on the food chain? Image of a cat looking
at a chart of the food chain that shows a can of cat food. Too complicated
to draw. Food chain. What's at the bottom? An amoeba? How does an
amoeba feel about that? It wants to preserve its self-esteem. The amoeba
thinks, "It may be the bottom link on the food chain, but it's still *my* link
on the food chain." Idea number eight.

Chain. Chains. Bondage and discipline freaks. Wouldn't they have had
a ball in a medieval torture chamber? Cliché cartoon image of the two
guys hanging by their hands from the prison wall. What does one say?
"This isn't doing much for my self-esteem." Idea number nine. Try a
switch on the same line. Who else might say it? Grass, cows, cats . . . dogs.
A dog, sitting in the "begging" position which its master has commanded
it to take, thinks, "This isn't doing much for my self-esteem." Make it

sharper. Substitute words. Have the dog *say* the line to the master. Dog, in begging position, says to master, "This isn't doing a hell of a lot for my self-esteem, you know." Finally, a workable dog and self-esteem notion. Idea number ten.

My pipe has gone out. Relight it. Pipes. Pipe smokers. Pipe smokers are supposed to be deep and reflective. What do they think about? Visual image of the usual cartoon thought balloon. What if the balloon were pipe smoke? A middle-aged pipe smoker sits alone. The pipe smoke thought balloon shows him thinking about a naked woman. His wife comes into the room. The balloon now shows him thinking deep thoughts: a quotation from Shakespeare, $E = mc^2$, the first line from *Moby-Dick* ("Call me Ishmael"), whatever. The wife leaves. He goes back to thinking about the naked woman. Idea number eleven.

Naked women. Lady Godiva. Godiva chocolates. Too much chocolate supposedly is bad for you. Is there a 12-step program for chocaholics? Chocolates. Candy. Candy kisses. Kisses. Kisses sweeter than wine. Wine. Brandy. Brandy casks on St. Bernard dogs doing rescue missions in the Alps. Stop there. A mental image of the dog. What else might the dog have hanging from its collar? Something more modern. A laptop computer? A cellular phone? Both viable cartoon concepts. Ideas number twelve and thirteen.

Cellular phones. Fancy telephone gadgetry. Digital numbers on phones. Push-button phones. Numbers you dial where a recorded voice asks you to punch another number, or several, before you get what you want. Infuriating, most of the time. How to fight back? A fat-cat, pompous tycoon says into his telephone, "Young lady, I do not feel I should have to push *any* button in order to speak to a live operator." Idea number fourteen.

"I am perfectly aware, Operator, that I may dial that number directly. I have no wish to do so, however."

The phone on the desk rings. It's somebody who will make a free estimate about the cost of putting aluminum shingles on the sides of the house. No more painting the outside of the building, ever. Hang up. Wish for a moment I'd made a smart aleck rejoinder, but couldn't think of one. Lost my train of thought. Grab a book of cartoons. The first one shows two angels standing on a cloud. Don't read the caption. What might they be talking about? Sex? Politics? Religion? Aluminum shingles? No help there. Put props in their hands. Maybe the usual: harps. Nothing comes from that. What other props might they have? Cellular phones. Put several angels in the picture, each one talking earnestly into a cellular phone. Funny. Doesn't need a caption. Idea number fifteen.

"Meow, meow, meow." The cat is really insistent now. Better feed it. It'll improve his self-esteem. Didn't get that idea straight. Got a workable notion about dogs and self-esteem, but nothing about cats and self-esteem, or *dogs and cats* and self-esteem. No strolling sousaphone player idea, either.

Maybe next time . . .

IV
Shop Talk About Cartooning

24
Harald Bakken Interviews
Mischa Richter

If the process of creating visual humor usually leaves us with additional topics and ideas that still need to be explored, so also did the process of creating this book. To discuss some of those additional topics and ideas, we decided to have Harald Bakken interview Mischa Richter about his extensive experience as a cartoonist. Appropriately enough, the interview took place on April Fool's Day.

You've been creating visual humor professionally for more than half a century, and you've worked in just about every aspect of the field. How did you get started in the visual humor business?

Mischa Richter: Cartooning has always appealed to me because I love to laugh, to draw, and to comment about the world we live in. For me, without a laugh, the day will never end. I was always drawing, as far back as when I was two years old. Later, when I was growing up in Russia, I even had a private teacher, an artist who came to the house and taught me how to draw. I lived in what is now the Ukraine during the Russian Revolution. There was a lot of political talk all around me. I thought that cartooning was a natural thing to do because I saw so much cartooning all around me, in newspapers, with people discussing various political movements.

When my family came to this country, I won a scholarship to the Museum School in Boston. I went there for a year and studied with Phillip Hale, who was the son of Edward Everett Hale. He looked just like the statue of his father in the Boston Public Garden. He always scared the hell out of me. I thought the statue was coming into the classroom. He was a very good painter and a very good teacher. Then I went on to Yale Art School. I thought that getting some kind of diploma or degree might prepare me for at least teaching, if nothing else happened. I enjoyed Yale because they had a wonderful history of art course, with slides. I didn't always agree with the professor because at that time, in the 1930s, the fellow teaching painting thought that art ended around the Victorian era and that nobody knew how to draw or paint after that. But it was very, very exciting to be there. And after I got out of Yale Art School, where there was such an emphasis on the history of art, I fell in love with mural painting because it had a direct communication with people. It wasn't dependent on special training to be able to look at it. I think all art is communication, and the faster it communicates, the happier everybody is—the viewer and the creator. To me, newspapers and magazines gave the quickest media for communicating. I saw no difference between making a good drawing for a magazine and making a good drawing or painting to hang on a wall. I still don't.

Unfortunately, many critics tend to think "high art here and popular art there and never the twain shall meet."

Mischa Richter: There are all kinds of people in cartooning, of course. Some of them who are very successful will say to you, "I'm not an artist." So there's a place for everybody. But in my particular case, I felt that there was no difference between composing a cartoon and composing a painting—any painting, whether abstract or nonabstract—because with anything on a flat surface like that, you're trying to make a point. Whether your point is plastic or plastic plus literary, you're still trying to make a point.

At any rate, that's how I began to draw cartoons. After I got out of school, magazines were going strong. It was during the Depression. While everybody stood in line to get something to eat in a soup kitchen, artists all around me were breaking the general rule about starving artists, because they were selling to magazines.

I started by going to New York every Wednesday. Wednesday, for some reason, was the day that the magazine editors looked at cartoon submissions. By getting off at Grand Central, I could cover *The Saturday Evening Post, The New Yorker, Colliers, This Week* magazine, *True* magazine, *Yankee* magazine, and so on. All of them were within three blocks of each other. And they were waiting for cartoonists to submit their work because they needed the cartoons. In doing the rounds on Wednesday, there were other cartoonists I met, and the whole thing became a very happy situation. We'd meet at noon in a restaurant somewhere. We'd go around. One fellow would say, "I got five OKs." Another would say, "I got three here." They paid $50 per drawing in those days, and you could get a pretty good apartment for $50 a month. So $50 a drawing was not a bad deal.

After selling these cartoons for a while, I got a contract with *PM* magazine to do political cartoons. Shortly after that, King Features asked me to do a daily newspaper panel. Soon after that *The New Yorker* took me on. I dropped the *PM* contract and kept the King Features and *New Yorker* contracts for many years together. Of course, I'm still with *The New Yorker*.

I grew up in the Midwest in the forties and fifties, in small towns. I started reading The New Yorker *when I was in high school in a little Minnesota town that had maybe two thousand people in it. I'm sure I wasn't what anybody at* The New Yorker *had in mind as their typical audience, if they even thought about a typical audience, but for me the magazine was a wonderful way into another world. I fell in love with* New Yorker *cartoons when I was about fifteen. People think of the* New Yorker *audience as being sophisticated and urban, and it certainly is that, but the magazine also had a lot of impact everywhere. What was it like to work with* The New Yorker *in those days—the forties and fifties?*

"*. . . and in conclusion, Mr. President, I say that if after this great war we are to have a federation of all nations of the earth, where would it be more fitting to have the seat of government of this great brotherhood of free and friendly peoples than right here in God's country?*"

Mischa Richter: An interesting thing about *The New Yorker* is the feeling of family and belonging that it created among all those that worked for it. I found myself in a situation where I had an acquaintance with James Thurber (once he even gave me a gag; he thought I was the right artist to draw the idea), where Harold Ross [the legendary *New Yorker* editor] was taking my work home to look it over to make sure that it was just right. All of a sudden I became part of the activity of all of these people. It was kind of like a ''hold my hand, I'm a stranger in paradise'' situation. I was very pleased.

The intimacy and concern the people in charge had for the people who worked for *The New Yorker* is something unique and very interesting. Ross used to say, for example, ''We're getting too much advertising. We're doing something wrong.'' [Laughter] And, in a way, he meant it. The success of *The New Yorker* was phenomenal. It had the highest subscription renewal rate of any magazine in those days and right up to the early sixties. I don't know what it is now, but it was true then. Its success sprang, I think, from a certain amount of an attitude that said, ''To hell with the bottom line, let's do what we believe is right and there will be enough people to recognize it.'' That formula worked. It's just amazing to me how successful they became in the commercial sense, while they still retained the intrinsic values that you only find in books you select yourself to buy in a bookstore. And the cartoon was one of the major forces in *The New Yorker*. Ross had great respect for cartoonists. You can see by the layout of the magazine what a force the cartoons became. The expression ''This is a *New Yorker* cartoon'' became a kind of synonym for quality in humor.

The other thing that made me feel good was that I was one of the first members of the Cartoonists' Society. Rube Goldberg was in it at that time, and Milton Caniff, and a few other people of that caliber in the comic-strip business. I was a new member, a little younger, certainly younger than Rube Goldberg. They were all very friendly and made me feel right at home. That was very nice.

As for the rest, I just worked on, that's all. And I had a very pleasant life doing it.

''Yes, son, we're Republican.''

How would you describe your general approach to the creation of humorous drawings?

Mischa Richter: Someone visiting a kindergarten asked a little girl how she went about making a drawing. She replied, "First I give a think, then I put a line around it." That marvelous answer cuts through all the phony and pretentious attempts to define art. However, a cartoonist has to give two thinks before putting a line around them. The first think is the idea, or gag. The second think is how to draw it. The only exception to this might be when a picture itself suggests an idea.

    There is nothing in the rules of the game that prevents a cartoonist from making the best drawing in the world. Most memorable cartoons survive by formal means alone. Their visual impact is so strong that we often forget the gag. However, the gag and drawing are so intertwined that we will never really know what came first, like the proverbial chicken and egg. For example, Daumier's lawyers, Uncle Sam, the Addams Family are powerful and memorable visual concepts, and yet without the gag that gave them life there would have been no laugh, no satire, no social comment, no historical record. When I first started working for *The New Yorker*, James Geraghty, who was then cartoon editor, would often tell me when rejecting a rough how much he liked the way it was drawn and how sorry he was that before he could use it in the magazine, it first had to have a gag. Lee Lorenz, who succeeded Geraghty as cartoon editor, feels the same way, I'm sure. When I was drawing my daily newspaper panel, "Strictly Richter," I often used gag men because I had to keep from four to six weeks ahead. But a cartoonist without a personal approach to humor—or in some rare cases without a sense of humor [Laughter]— couldn't recognize a salable idea submitted by a gag writer. That's very important. You've got to be a gag man yourself to be able to use gag men.

    It's important to remember too that in a humorous drawing the face sets the pace. If you see someone frowning at you, or looking like hell, you don't feel funny anymore.

Whenever I work on a finish, I become a stage, TV, and movie director. I cast the characters, select the props, position the actors, and make sure that the punch or surprise ending is, in most cases, placed on the right. I position the surprise ending there because we read that way, from left to right. I frequently bring to mind what Harold Ross, the *New Yorker* editor, used to ask when he looked at a drawing. Ross always wanted to know "where is it, what is happening, and who is doing the talking?"

Can you say a little more about how you're like a stage or TV or movie director?

Mischa Richter: The cast of characters and the rest of it comes from the script, which is the gag. I fool around with the placement of things to see what would give the fastest delivery of the gag. A gag is always a surprise. When you're trying to surprise someone, whether it's just talking or pulling a trick on them on April Fool's Day—since today is April first— you lead them into a situation first where they're comfortable, and then disturb that comfort by introducing an element that is the surprise. And then they laugh.

I think you should start with the familiar, particularly in drawing, because, unlike a writer who can introduce you for two or three chapters

"And today in Washington a top Administration apologist issued an apology while denying that there was anything to apologize for."

*"Just for today, you call me Oberon and I'll call you Titania.
Nobody else has to know."*

to what he or she is writing about and then begin to dwell on what comes from that, an artist doesn't have that luxury. The familiar helps the speed. Also, the familiar immediately deals with subjects that most people think about, like marriage—that's, of course, the most common subject.

I think the familiar also includes the emotions that people are familiar with. A desert island isn't a setting people know, but being lonely is a familiar experience. The familiarity of the emotion draws people into a desert island cartoon right away.

Mischa Richter: Yes.

What elements go into a really good cartoon drawing?

Mischa Richter: To me it's a drawing that does not interfere with the speed and clarity of the idea it portrays. It's safe to say that we recognize it when we see it.

Have you seen what I guess we might call the "visual language" of cartooning change over the years?

Mischa Richter: Yes. My feeling is that the change is due to the influence of another field, which is moviemaking, animation, and so on. Cartoon animation has created its own drawing calligraphy. The artist-animator

"Not the Bermuda triangle?"

has to draw the same characters over and over again, changing each drawing slightly to create motion. In most cases, this translates into simpler, linear drawings, almost like handwriting. This applies to most comic strips too. The visual impact of this kind of influence in drawing is very powerful because it's used on television. Regrettably, the publishing field hasn't escaped its influence. The method of drawing for animation doesn't fit in or blend gracefully in a foreign environment like a magazine or book, which has its own visual world. I feel that a magazine or a book is a more contemplative medium in the sense that you can look at it carefully, think about it. So there's no reason for not putting in a scratchy line or a lightened shade, which could be eliminated in a newspaper or an animated cartoon. In a way, magazine cartoons and book drawings are like a gallery of paintings and drawings reduced to a smaller scale. Comic strips are a great American art form, but dealing with magazine cartooning is another story, so you shouldn't mix the two together.

You've done a single-panel syndicated newspaper feature, you've done magazine cartoons, you've done spots, you've done magazine illustration, you've done children's books, and you've done advertising. Do you work differently depending on the kind of medium you're drawing for?

Mischa Richter: I think I do subconsciously because, as in all art, the problem that you're trying to solve springs from where this problem is going to have to be solved, whether it's in a newspaper or a magazine, or a spot in the *New York Times*. Somehow, the field you're working in—by field I mean the actual area, almost like real estate—creates its own techniques. I think it's true in music too. Ballet music is different from something else. I think every creative person is influenced by the problems he or she has to solve.

Can you give an example of that—maybe take something you've done recently where the particular medium or genre you were working in influenced the way you solved the problem?

Mischa Richter: In the book illustration that I've been doing in recent days, for some reason I feel that I can let myself go more. I don't know why, but I feel a little freer. Maybe it's just that I'm getting older and a lot of people, if they've worked in a medium for years, feel more relaxed in it and let themselves go. Maybe they know more about it and instinctively understand what the problem is. When I did "Strictly Richter," I was very much influenced by the printed page around the feature. I was very conscious of black against white. I was trying to solve the problem of the formal means, like the abstract painters, in the sense that you need to place a black here and a white there and a gray there—only the placement of those values has to do with expressing a literal idea rather than a purely visual idea. So I combined the two. And all my panels for King Features

"Push the Scotch salmon with dill sauce."

years ago, if I say so myself, stood out. They punched you right in the face as you looked at them. All art, in order to function, has to come out and grab you. It doesn't wait for you to come in and grab it. If you're an artist, you're on the spot. You have to be like a fighter, coming out and giving it all you've got.

I was interested in what you said earlier about a drawing not interfering with the cartoon's idea. Can you talk a little more about that?

Mischa Richter: The speed with which the viewer recognizes the gag is the essence. If the drawing is bad, for those who are aware of the drawing, those who are sensitive to drawing, it interferes. They say, "Oh, what a lousy drawing," then they say "Oh, it's a pretty good idea" and kind of laugh. But I feel that *nothing* should interfere. There should be a good drawing, a good idea, everything working together, a perfect marriage of all these elements.

I've worked some in the theater. In the theater you do a lot of things with visual images and motion. If the audience is ever consciously aware of what you're doing, you're not doing it right. But, at the same time, if you don't do it right, the audience is very aware that something is wrong, even if they can't put a finger on it.

Mischa Richter: This has to do with direction, the placement of things. In fact, years ago I talked with Mike Gordon, the guy who directed the movie *Pillow Talk.* He studied the old masters, just as I did—the mural paintings and the storytelling. They were done to tell a story to a mostly illiterate population, and so the story began on the left and moved to the right. Gordon said, "I do that too when I direct. I want the action to start somewhere and then end on the right, if possible." That was very interesting. Both of us went to Yale. He went to Yale Drama School and I went to Yale Art School. So maybe living in New Haven had something to do with it. [Laughter]

Because drawings are fixed in space as opposed to, say, movies, people generally don't think of drawing as having motion, but obviously it's terribly important, particularly in cartoons, that they do have motion.

Mischa Richter: Oh, I think all good drawing has motion—all good paintings and, for that matter, good music. That's why Mozart is so good. When you think that every possible chord variation has been done, he does one more. And that creates the motion. The essence of all good art in any medium is not to bore anybody. If you bore people, you're finished. And motion kills boredom.

Let's return to The New Yorker *for a minute, and talk about the content of cartoons.* The New Yorker *has some limits on the material it will publish. For example, it doesn't do graphic sexual material. But, with a few exceptions, you can do just about anything for the magazine. You can draw animals, you can do political material, you can publish domestic cartoons, you can use a variety of artistic techniques.*

Mischa Richter: I was never restricted, and neither was anyone else, in commenting on current events. I never really went for a strictly political cartoon to begin with, because if you don't like someone, you can make a funny face on them, and that doesn't prove anything. What proves something is an argument. If you present a basic argument against something in a drawing, or make fun of the position that the other party takes in a logical way or an undeniable way, then that creates a kind of political statement without the drawing really becoming what is known as a political cartoon. I don't believe any political cartoon actually changed

"Your Majesty, Mr. President, Your Eminence, Your Royal Highness, Mr. Ambassador, Madam Chairperson, Your Excellency, distinguished clergy, most gracious host, fellow-delegates, loyal supporters, comrades-in-arms, honorable fellows, most generous sponsors, honored patrons, distinguished guests, kind friends, fellow-countrymen, ladies and gentlemen—And now I see my time is up."

anything. I know political cartoonists have been persecuted. Daumier was, and so on. But that's many years ago. I don't think cartoons change many people today. Whatever they believe, they believe, in spite of the drawings.

Can you say a little more about the difference between political satire and strictly political—or, perhaps, more accurately, editorial—cartoons?

Mischa Richter: *The New Yorker* is very careful about that. I once had a drawing of the President and his cabinet. There's no point in saying which president it was, but it was a few years ago. The President was saying, "Anybody got any ideas?" It seemed funny at the time. But it was never published. They were playing around with "Shall we, or shall we not, use the face of the President?" And they didn't use it. However, during the Russian May Day parade, I had a drawing that ran full page in *The New Yorker* of all the Soviet dignitaries on the reviewing stand above Lenin's tomb. In the parade there were balloons of Mickey Mouse up in the air. One of the guys was saying to the other, "Détente!"* That was a funny idea. It was reprinted a lot, including in the *New York Times*. For that particular period, that seemed appropriate. That's a political statement that is really nonpolitical. But it is amusing.

One of the things that your approach to political subjects does is keep the satire from being dated. If you have an editorial cartoon that shows a particular president or a particular candidate, it may be funny at that moment, but the humor is gone the next. I think, for example, about Daumier's drawings. He did some specific people. But when you see his lawyers acting self-important, or his politicians trying to soft-soap a voter, they're as contemporary as if he'd drawn them yesterday. By staying general, you're more timeless.

Mischa Richter: Well, I did mention specific people now and then, but in a way that doesn't hurt them. Once I had a couple of guys in the bar talking and one said, "Isn't it about time we stopped blaming Alf Landon for everything?" Now, Alf Landon asked for this cartoon. He loved it. He had it in his house. When I looked at a film of him, I could see the cartoon right on his desk. So there was a comment that was kind yet political. I never mentioned President Reagan, but one cartoon *The New Yorker* bought during his administration was a TV announcer who's saying, "And now, the charming President of the United States." There are many others, but I believe they're kind of gentle.

---

*See page 116.

"Ladies and gentlemen, the charming President of the United States."

You said to me once—I don't think altogether seriously—that one of the reasons you got into cartooning was that in some ways you thought life was a joke, or at least that you had a take on life that saw the absurd in it. How much do you think that's true?

Mischa Richter: I don't think life is a joke. But—maybe I'm nuts—unless people are interfering in my life, I feel good most of the time. You have to feel good to do cartoons. There are formulas, but basically you have to feel that it's fun. Maybe it's due to the fact that I'm an only child and always felt secure with my parents. My father was very good about encouraging me to draw. I wasn't exposed to the kind of suffering that a lot of people may have been, even though I lived in the midst of the Ten Days That Shook the World.

There's a myth that humorists all had unhappy childhoods and are all somehow compensating for that. Obviously there are some people who did and do, but I don't think that's the real story.

Mischa Richter: No. I was fortunate. I felt very secure. The Revolution looked like some kind of a show going on outside the gates of the property where we lived. There were bad guys and good guys, and there was a lot of idealism and a lot of cruelty, but to me—in my stupid way when I was a child—all of it was show business. That's because my father would come home and everything would be all right. Of course, as far as

"Miss Wilcox, get me the Coast."

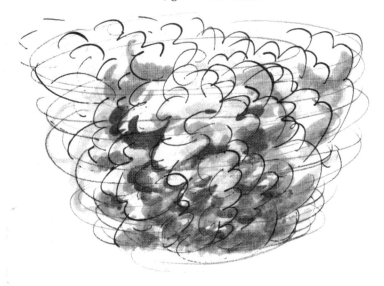

the actual physical end of it, in those days there were no bombings of civilians. Battles were fought outside the city. There was no house-to-house fighting. None of that existed in my city. And so things were kind of settled outside. Whoever won came in and marched through the main streets.

At one point, we were talking about how an artist develops a "style"—since I'm primarily a writer, I'd say how, as an artist, you "find your own voice." Can you cast your mind back to the beginning of your career and say something about how you came to understand what it was that became the Mischa Richter style?

Mischa Richter: You mean composition?

Partly I mean composition. But not just composition. The whole business. Viewers see one of your drawings and they can say, even without looking at the signature, "That's a Mischa Richter drawing."

Mischa Richter: My philosophy was that I never strove for style because I felt that, just as your handwriting is very personal, your style evolves naturally. We're all different, and that difference will come out in the style. Some styles are more exciting than others, but the difference will come out. So I never pushed for style.

Putting down a line creates a physical excitement for me, just like some of the Japanese brush strokes. I like to feel the line, the excitement of telegraphing the line from my head to my hand to the pen to the paper. I get a great deal of pleasure from that. Sometimes I feel the need before I start to do a little warm-up with my body, that is, to move my arms a little bit, to imagine myself moving around a little bit, to get into that rhythm that an athlete does when he or she tunes up before running.

Or the way a musician tunes up.

Mischa Richter: Yes. Just a little tune-up, like I once saw Rachmaninoff do, nervously adjusting his coattails before hitting the first note.

Actors do that too. They warm up their voices and their bodies. And I know what you mean by the physical excitement of having your hands do something. I didn't feel that so much as a writer. But when I started to create music, I found that the way I compose is with my hands on the piano keyboard. I don't think it in my head and then play it. I play it and then I hear if it's any good, if it's worth writing down.

Mischa Richter: Yes. Because you know it's all an extension of yourself.

That's it. I think that's the most wonderful thing. You draw on just about all the resources you have, at some point at least, not necessarily for every sentence or every song or every drawing.

Mischa Richter: When you do a drawing over and over again if you're not satisfied, and finally get one you like, you don't quite know why it's better than the others. But somehow it flows throughout as though it's one continuous line rather than a series of hiccups and burps that kind of work together, but don't really accomplish anything.

I think about that for scenes in plays or movies too. When you're doing one, you can write each line perfectly, speak it perfectly, do each gesture perfectly, but then there's a point at which something else happens, and that's what makes it a great scene instead of a series of well-delivered lines or well-delivered gestures. There's absolutely nothing better than when you know that's what has happened. Still, I find the process a little mystifying. To me there's always a little sense of "Hmmm! My goodness!" when something works.

Mischa Richter: Yes. "Where did it come from?" Well, that's why writing ideas, as you do and I do and we both do together—it's the mystery of it that's exciting. All the talking you can do about the creative process still leaves you hanging in the sense that the actual mystery of what makes something better than something else *is* a mystery. An art teacher can lead you to the water, but he can't make you drink. Why does a simple idea work? You say "Why didn't I think of it right away? Where did it come from?"

It's supposed to surprise the viewer, but in fact . . .

Mischa Richter: . . . it surprises me.

Yes. And thank goodness for that.

Mischa Richter: But then comes the next thing that bothers you. After you latch onto something that works, you say, "Well, why can't I think of a variation?" And it doesn't work.

That's the downside of it—the times when you think you're doing exactly what you've always done and nothing happens.

Mischa Richter: Why was it good then?

Exactly. Let me ask you a different kind of question. What major changes have you seen over the years in cartooning?

Mischa Richter: The outstanding change, of course, is the demise of so many magazines. That made it a narrower field. That's the major change. There is some change in humor itself. Personally, I find that a lot of it nowadays is very mean and tasteless, not at all concerned with the human condition, which is to me one of the wealthiest sources for a cartoonist. Cartooning really gives you a wonderful chance to comment. But you

"Before we give our verdict, Judge, would you care to hear something really novel in twelve part harmony?"

could reverse this argument and say that no comment about the human condition is also a social statement. So where are you? Corner of Fifth and Main. [Laughter]

How about changes in the subject matter of cartoons? One thing I can think of is that now there are certain characters that just don't get used, like the chorus girl who's on the make for the older man, or the older man who's on the make for the chorus girl.

Mischa Richter: Obviously there are girlie magazines now. I remember submitting girlie gags to *The New Yorker* that in the past would have been funny, but they said "We're not going to publish them. Why should we publish them when there are other magazines doing that specifically?" And, of course, women's lib has made an impact too. And the boss . . . the boss is still made fun of, but not quite in the same way as he used to be. Look at the old movies—the black and white movies—and you'll see the changes. It's analogous. There are not as many psychiatrists either.

That's interesting.

Mischa Richter: You've noticed that?

It is true.

Mischa Richter: In the old days, you could just put someone on the couch and have him say anything to a psychiatrist and it was funny. Today editors are a little more selective about those gags. I don't know why. Maybe they've given up—given up on psychoanalyzing anybody.

The world has gone mad, so why bother?

Mischa Richter: Yes. In fact, someone once sent me an idea—I could never sell it—that had a psychiatrist's convention with a sign saying "Legalize Mental Health." [Laughter]

What advice would you give to someone who wants to begin to work in this field?

Mischa Richter: First, I'd say, "Remember, you are unique. There is no one like you, nor will there ever be." In the final analysis, that quality that makes you different from others is what makes your ideas and your drawings. That's important. And that quality is the element that will interest the editors. Editors don't necessarily know what they want. Often your ideas and drawings will create a new and exciting addition for the publication you are submitting to. Remember too that while you need the editors, they also need you. It's like a bank, you know. People are awed by bankers. But bankers need your money in order for them to make money.

Remember, too, that cartooning is in constant demand by various media. And cartoons adorn not only refrigerator doors, but museum walls as well. Cartoonists have the excitement of "now" as well as the challenge of "forever."

Then I'd say, "If you don't feel that you *must* do it, don't get into it." That's the way I feel. I never made a choice. I just continued the way I always lived. I think that's true of any art. And it should be fun. Fun is contagious. See how some comedians laugh when they tell their jokes because they're enjoying it so much. I think that's important. And I think that's a common denominator for all creative work—in some way, it's fun to do.

V
Where to Read More

"In a moment we'll have a few words by the chairman of the board. But first, Mahler's Eighth Symphony."

Selected Bibliography

A quick search through the catalogue of any good-sized library will yield the titles of many books that deal with the technical aspects of cartooning. We mention here only a few books and periodicals that we have found particularly useful in the creation of ideas for visual humor.

Cartoonists Guild. *The Art in Cartooning: Seventy-five Years of American Magazine Cartoons*. Edited by Edwin Fisher, Mort Gerberg, and Ron Wolin. New York: Charles Scribner's Sons, 1975.

A survey of American magazine cartooning from the 1890s through the 1970s.

Chase's Annual Events: The Day-by-Day Directory. Chicago: Contemporary Books.

Published yearly. Directory of several thousand holidays, anniversaries, birthdays, special events, and so on, with entries for every day of the year. Useful for writing seasonal material.

Comedy Calendar Guide. Published by Gag Recap Publications, Box 774, Bensalem, PA 19020.

Mimeographed pamphlet that lists stimuli for the creation of ideas for all of the major seasonal holidays and events.

Evans, Ivor H., ed. *Brewer's Dictionary of Phrase & Fable.* New York: Harper & Row, 1981.

Classic dictionary of literary, mythical, and artistic references, fables, common phrases, etc. A gold mine for a visual humorist. (If you forget the names of the Seven Deadly Sins or the Seven Wonders of the World or the Seven Hills of Rome, this is the place to look.)

Gag Recap. Published by Gag Recap Publications, Box 774, Bensalem, PA 19020.

Published monthly. Summarizes each cartoon published in most major American magazines.

Murrell, William. *A History of American Graphic Humor.* 2 vols. Volume 1: 1747–1865. Volume 2: 1865-1938. New York: Cooper Square Publishers, 1967.

A valuable survey of graphic humor in America from the colonial period through the early twentieth century.

Rogers, James. *The Dictionary of Clichés.* New York: Facts on File Publications, 1985.

More than 2,000 clichés. Will help you to remember 2,000 or 20,000 more.

The New Yorker Album of Drawings, 1925–1975. New York: Viking Penguin Books, 1975.

New Yorker cartoons from the magazine's first fifty years.

The New Yorker Cartoon Album, 1975–1985. New York: Viking Press, 1985.

New Yorker cartoons from a more recent period.

The New Yorker Twenty-Fifth Anniversary Album: 1925–1950. New York: Harper & Row, 1951. Perennial Library (paperback edition), 1986.

New Yorker cartoons from the magazine's early history.

Writer's Digest Books. *Humor and Cartoon Markets.* Available from *Writer's Digest,* 1507 Dana Ave., Cincinnati, OH 45207.

Yearly listing of markets for visual and other kinds of humor.